# apartment therapy
## complete + happy home

**MAXWELL RYAN & JANEL LABAN
WITH HEATHER SUMMERVILLE**

AND THE EDITORS OF APARTMENT THERAPY

Photographs by Melanie Acevedo
Illustrations by Meghann Stephenson

potter style
new york

Published in the United States by Potter Style, an imprint of the
Crown Publishing Group, a division of Penguin Random House
LLC, New York.
www.crownpublishing.com
www.potterstyle.com

POTTER STYLE is a trademark and POTTER with colophon is a
registered trademark of Penguin Random House LLC.

Library of Congress Cataloging-in-Publication Data
is available upon request.

ISBN 978-0-7704-3445-8
eBook ISBN 978-0-7704-3446-5

Printed in China

Cover and book design by Ashley Tucker
Illustrations by Meghann Stephenson
Cover photography by Melanie Acevedo

10 9 8 7 6 5 4 3 2 1

First Edition

To our loyal readers
and the lovely, talented,
and hardworking staff
at Apartment Therapy

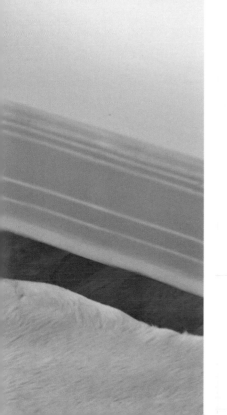

# contents

# introduction

"Having a warm home that looks good and works well, and that you and your family and friends enjoy, must be one of the most worthwhile things in life . . . "

—TERENCE CONRAN, *The House Book*, 1974

Decorating is something lovely that you see, but it is something you should *feel* too. A complete and happy home is so much more than a series of pretty rooms.

At Apartment Therapy, we've spent more than ten years visiting remarkable homes around the world. In that time, we've managed to document the uniqueness, authenticity, and aspirations of a whole new generation. Thousands of homes have been photographed, their great ideas and ingenious resources recorded in detail, so that we could share it all with you on a daily basis.

Now we want to put everything we've learned about decorating, organizing, cleaning, and repairs between two covers you can hold in your hands. Call us old-fashioned, but we do believe that books capture experiences in a completely different way than what we do each day on the web. So we embarked on this journey, photographing beautiful and unique places from coast to coast, to make sure you have everything you need to make and maintain a fabulous home.

## how this book works . . .

This book is divided into three sections, starting with "Setting Up Your Home," which walks you through the early stages of getting settled: how to move in, choose your style, plan a room, and figure out all the final finishes—from wall paint to curtains to flooring and more. The "Living in Your Home" section will inspire you with photographs of some of the most amazing rooms we've found from New York to Texas, Chicago to LA. They are all different, personal, and packed with ideas to share. We end with "Maintaining Your Home," a hardworking section filled with tips, sources, and guidelines on how to clean, organize, and repair just about anything.

Here is our biggest book to date. We hope it will inspire you to create a beautiful, organized space that you can enjoy with family and friends.

Welcome to your happy home.

**CHICAGO**
Eric Oliver + Thea Goodman
Professor + Author
daughter, Esme + son, Ethan

## Go find your home in a place you love . . .

We like to believe we can make a home anywhere. Typically, the farther you are from a city the more space you'll get. Never forget, though, that even more than square footage, the three things that matter most when finding a home are . . . location, location, location.

How far you are from friends and family will influence how "at home" you feel. Take this to heart, and choose a place as close as you can to the neighborhood and people you want to be near. Also, keep in mind that the spaces outside your door are an extension of your home. You'll live in these areas as much as you will inside your house. So no matter how "perfect" a home might appear, if the land it sits on is problematic, it won't be perfect in the long run.

What should you spend? Unlike in many other areas of life, it's always a good idea to stretch when buying a home. How far should you stretch? That's a very personal decision, but spending a little more (between 10 and 20 percent) can often make a big difference. Be aspirational. Remember, you want room to grow, so aim for a space that's a little bigger, a little nicer, and a little better located than you may have originally intended. It will pay off in the end, because it inspires you to work harder for a home you're excited to live in.

If you have it in you to take on a fixer-upper, there's no better way to save money. Regular people can be lazy, but Apartment Therapy people take on challenges—and there's great value in that. With a little style and elbow grease, any home can be transformed for far less than if you bought it done. The DIY route allows you to add your own character from the get-go.

# 1

## the
## home
## hunt

LOS ANGELES
**Ruthie Sommers + Luke McDonough**
Interior Designer + CEO, Air Media
daughters Eloise, Bailey, Posey

## the craftsman bungalow

**WHAT'S TO LOVE:** Hallmarks include wide front porches, open floor plans, and loads of built-in charm (exposed beams, custom woodwork). These (typically) one-and-a-half-story homes have roots dating back to the Arts and Crafts movement.

**WHAT YOU SHOULD KNOW:** Space is limited, with most bungalows clocking in at 1,000 square feet or fewer. Older (unrenovated) homes often have small closets and only one bathroom.

## the split-level

**WHAT'S TO LOVE:** These multilevel homes induce *Brady Bunch* nostalgia on sight. Designed to separate living functions by floor, they offer lots of privacy and noise control.

**WHAT YOU SHOULD KNOW:** Though split-levels have lots of rooms, they tend to be small—and the mazelike floor plan makes renovating costly. Curb appeal can be an issue, too, with uneven window placement and out-of-scale roofs.

## the tudor

**WHAT'S TO LOVE:** The steeply pitched roofs and decorative half-timber framing are the stuff of fairy-tale castles. Massive chimneys and large casement windows add to the charming facade, while inside, decorative details are echoed throughout.

**WHAT YOU SHOULD KNOW:** Because the floor plan is typically dictated by an aesthetically pleasing exterior, rooms can be small and choppy—especially upstairs, where ceilings tend to have a slope.

# common house styles

You've settled on your dream location—and now you're ready to start the home hunt. Our quick guide to housing styles breaks down the pros and cons of some of the most popular types on the market.

## the modern high-rise

**WHAT'S TO LOVE:** Most new-construction buildings have window walls, which mean plenty of sunlight. Open designs focus on an increased living area, so kitchens and living rooms often share a bigger space.

**WHAT YOU SHOULD KNOW:** To compensate for the large living area, bedrooms and storage spaces are typically small. Finishings can be on the cheaper side, so it's always worth paying extra attention to those during your hunt.

## the mid-century ranch

**WHAT'S TO LOVE:** Hugely popular in the '50s and '60s, this long, single-story style is known for its compact-[...] open floor plan. Today, they're being snapped up and renovated into modern, green homes at a minimal co[...]

**WHAT YOU SHOULD KNOW:** They can appear plain and dated unless spruced up with architectural flourishes. Numerous ground-level windows can present a secur[...] issue in certain locations.

## the colonial

**WHAT'S TO LOVE:** Easily spotted by its symmetrical exterior (a centrally placed door flanked by evenly placed windows) and overall grandness, this two- to three-story style is one of the most common—and sought-after—housing types.

**WHAT YOU SHOULD KNOW:** Bigger homes equal bigger utility bills, especially in older colonials running on outdated heating systems. Upgrading to an efficient HVAC system is necessary.

## the row house (or brownstone)

**WHAT'S TO LOVE:** These city buildings often feature original architectural details, like ceiling medallions and decorative molding. By urban standards, they have a lot of living space divided vertically among multiple floors.

**WHAT YOU SHOULD KNOW:** Because owning an entire row house is pricey, a lot of these buildings have been split into multiple units (one or two per floor), often with a railroad-style layout. Size and privacy come at a premium.

## the modern green home

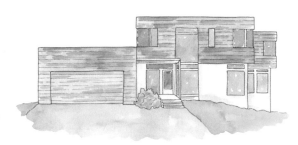

**WHAT'S TO LOVE:** Wide-open floor plans offer lots of flexibility, and the eco-minded design translates to sweeping views. Highly efficient HVAC systems leave a smaller footprint on the planet (and your bank account).

**WHAT YOU SHOULD KNOW:** All that glass and concrete can come off as sterile and cold. Using reclaimed materials for building will require more frequent upkeep. And large windows make privacy a consideration.

# countdown to a **stress-free moving day**

## 4 weeks to go

- ○ CONFIRM YOUR MOVE-IN DATE. Give your landlord written notice if you've been renting.
- ○ START PLANNING. Work on basic floor plans to determine what you need to bring—and what you can get rid of.
- ○ RESEARCH MOVERS or make a truck rental reservation.
- ○ SET UP OUT-BOXES (one per room) for belongings you won't be taking with you. Be tough! Fewer items mean a smoother move—and lighter life in your new place.
- ○ START SELLING. If you plan to sell items online, take good photos and get them listed.

## 3 weeks to go

- ○ STOCK UP ON PACKING MATERIALS. Buy, beg, or borrow plenty of boxes.
- ○ START PACKING. Getting nonessential items boxed up early is super-efficient and a great stress reliever.
- ○ UPDATE YOUR ADDRESS on all accounts and subscriptions.
- ○ SET UP A CHANGE OF ADDRESS/FORWARDING REQUEST with the post office.
- ○ TAKE ARTWORK DOWN from the walls, wrap or pack it safely, and patch the holes.

## 2 weeks to go

- ○ REQUEST TIME OFF. Give your employer your new address.
- ○ MAKE PACKING YOUR NEW HOBBY. If an item isn't essential at this point, it should be in a box.
- ○ GET UTILITIES IN ORDER. Arrange cancellations or transfers.
- ○ EMPTY YOUR OUT-BOXES. Donate, give things to friends, or set items outside with a FREE sign.
- ○ PLAN MEALS FOR THE NEXT WEEK to finish off perishables you won't be taking with you.

## moving week

- ○ SAY YOUR GOOD-BYES TO NEIGHBORS, and arrange for someone to keep an eye out for packages or important mail that might arrive after you've moved.
- ○ PACK UP EVERYTHING BUT THE ABSOLUTE ESSENTIALS: bedding, toiletries, a place setting or two, a change of clothes, phone/computer chargers, etc. Set aside a box to toss these things into on moving day.
- ○ CLEAN AS YOU GO THIS WEEK, leaving a few hours for a thorough cleaning the day before you move.
- ○ RETURN KEYS. If you've been renting, hand over your keys, arrange for your security deposit to be returned, and provide a forwarding address to your landlord.
- ○ RELAX. Order in, and enjoy your first night in your new home. It's the beginning of many good memories to come!

Flow is the biggest secret to creating a healthy, beautiful home.

## 2

# getting the right flow

Drawn from feng shui (China) and Vastu-sastra (India), *flow* refers to the way rooms allow people and energy to move in and around them. When a room is laid out well, it not only works better, looks good, and is easy to maintain; it is also more energetic. To put it more succinctly: it will make you happy.

Unhealthy flow happens when energy is directed in a straight line; let's call this **"bowling-alley syndrome."** Furniture lines the walls, and the center of the room is hollowed out, so you rush straight through a space, noticing nothing.

Bad flow also occurs when energy gets trapped. Think of this as **"pack-rat syndrome."** Too much furniture is crowded into a room, blocking access to certain areas.

A **healthy energy flow** meanders, gently curving and moving forward to reach all the corners of a room. This is what you want to design for. The goal is to have multiple routes through a space, without blocking windows or doorways.

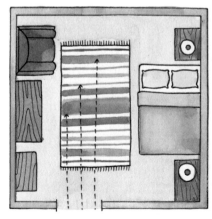

BOWLING-ALLEY SYNDROME

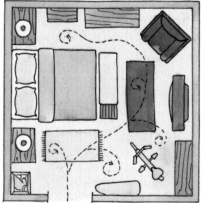

PACK-RAT SYNDROME

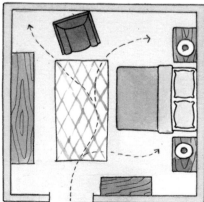

HEALTHY ENERGY FLOW

AUSTIN
Erin Williamson + Ben Roy
Interior Designer + Software Engineer
sons Ike, Luke

# the good flow guide

Every home is different. Each has its own set of issues, whether awkwardly shaped floor plans or teeny-tiny rooms. But a few overarching rules will help you set up your space with as much good flow as your square footage allows.

**bedroom:** The bed should be perpendicular to the wall and centered, so you can reach it from either side.

**living room:** Try pulling the sofa away from the wall. Creating a path behind it allows access to the fourth wall and helps you avoid "bowling-alley syndrome."

**dining room:** The table should not touch a wall, so all sides are available for seating. It's also a good idea to leave enough room for people to walk between the wall and the back of your dining chairs when— and this is the important part—the chair is pulled away from the table (as if you were standing up).

**kitchen:** Much of the makeup of this room is immobile, but if you have the flexibility to choose where your appliances go, pay particular attention to how they open. Be sure the oven door doesn't open into the dishwasher, and always adjust your refrigerator's hinges so that its doors open toward the closest wall.

## virtual floor-planning tools (let your fingers do the heavy lifting)

**FLOORPLANNER**
**floorplanner.com**
Draw a floor plan (or upload one to trace), then choose from a library of furniture and design items to play around with. The first project is free; after that you'll need to upgrade to a Plus or Pro account.

**AUTODESK HOMESTYLER**
**homestyler.com**
Select from loads of existing floor plans and add your own details—doors, windows, furniture, actual brand-name appliances, even paint colors (over 40,000 options)—for free. Bonus: It tracks material usage (flooring, paint), so you know how much to buy.

**FLOOR PLAN CREATOR**
**Google Play App**
With this free app you can start with a predefined room or draw your own. Symbols for doors, windows, furniture, and other details make it easy to use on a smartphone or tablet. *Note:* It's worth purchasing the add-on that allows you to sync to your cloud and share between devices.

**ROOMSCAN PRO**
**iTunes App**
Step away from your measuring tape! For a small fee this app allows you to "draw" accurate floor plans—accounting for windows and doors—by tapping your phone against every wall. You get measurements in minutes.

**E-DESIGNERS**
Talented interior designers, including Hilary Unger in New York City (buymyeye.net), offer floor-planning services virtually. Ask if they'll do *just* furniture planning, so you don't pay for services you don't need. On average, small rooms start at $450—but research designers in your area.

## divided rooms

The sofa is your most powerful tool in dictating a room's flow. Here, it creates a "wall," splitting the living and dining spaces. The rug is centered on the fireplace, emphasizing the room's width.

**IDEAL IF YOU WANT:** separate eating and living areas; a fireplace that's the center of attention.

**FLOW:** meanders in and around the living area, following the direction of the rug.

## angled room

It's refreshing to work outside a room's typical right angles. Here, the sofa and rug face the fireplace, but they're rocked 45 degrees to create some surprising views.

**IDEAL IF YOU WANT:** a room that's cozy and unconventional.

**FLOW:** nice and open, from the dining room (left) to the windows (right) with interesting routes between seating.

# one room, four ways

Sometimes a major room update is just a few strategic furniture moves away. Proof in point: we used the same basic components to reconfigure this space.

# one big room

The location of the sofa closes this room off—as opposed to the openness of the "adjacent" scenario—so it feels more cozy. The rug is turned horizontally (in line with the hearth) to emphasize the length of the room and pull the long space together.

**IDEAL IF YOU WANT:** open space but a less formal arrangement.

**FLOW:** with the back of the sofa facing the windows, the flow snakes between the living and dining areas, connecting the two at multiple points.

# adjacent rooms

The rug is flipped horizontally (and left slightly off-center from the hearth) to highlight the openness of this space. The sofa faces the fireplace, grounding a lovely, semiformal seating area. And the easy movement between living and dining rooms allows for chairs to be added and subtracted between spaces.

**IDEAL IF YOU WANT:** versatile seating for entertaining; a formal space centered on the fireplace.

**FLOW:** multiple entry and exit points, with winding paths that lead from the dining table straight through to the side windows (right).

What's your style? The short answer is, whatever makes you feel good.

Style is often hard to label—and it's going to be something you're constantly discovering. So when you start thinking about style in your home, never look at it as something that's "fixed." Enjoy shifting, tweaking, and experimenting with every room.

In our first book, *Apartment Therapy: The Eight-Step Home Cure,* we coined the terms Bones, Breath, Heart, and Head to outline the elements that define a room. Understanding them is a stepping-stone to finding and building your style. The goal is to get the foundations, Bones and Breath, squared away, and then focus on the Heart and Head.

Bones are the hard shell of a room: the walls, floors, ceiling, and built-in fixtures. You want to make sure they are all clean, painted or sealed, and in good repair.

Breath is the furniture arrangement. Establishing good flow in every room is key. (See chapter 2 for more on flow.)

The Heart is where style comes into play. It includes all the emotional touches: color, texture, shape, and pattern. These are the first things people notice in a room, so you should experiment to see what feels right.

The Head takes into account details that express your higher purpose, such as religious accessories and family pictures. While technically not a "style" element, they are symbols of your deepest beliefs and will color your home.

Of course, living with someone else means accounting for their (sometimes conflicting) tastes, too. Our advice? Reach a consensus on the first two levels (Bones and Breath); then allow space in every room for each person to express different Heart and Head elements. If your styles truly clash, divvy up the rooms by person—and enjoy sharing them with each other.

**3**

## style

**EAST HAMPTON, NY**
Christiane Lemieux + Joshua Young
Founder, DwellStudio + Real Estate Developer
daughter, Isabelle + son, William

## eclectic collector

A design mashup of personal treasures influenced by travel, functional design, and aesthetic passions.

### COLORS
Often bold and bright but can slip into neutral territory if it helps highlight the decorative eye candy.

### ELEMENTS
By its nature, this style is undefined. It's all about the mix! Layered prints, patterns, and textures.

### INFLUENCES
Global design, film, and art with a strong sense of individual style.

## happy modern

The sunny side of modern. Bright and joyful, with an appreciation and eye for design.

### COLORS
Saturated brights, chalky pastels, black, white, and clear.

### ELEMENTS
Bold patterns, lighter wood tones, painted wood finishes, plastic, cotton, paper, and felt.

### INFLUENCES
Scandinavian design. Mid-century modern. Pop culture.

## style DNA

Pinpoint your design aesthetic (most likely a mix of one or two—or more!— broad "looks") with a quick study of these eight styles.

# classic glam

The modern way to work with classic elements is to pick and choose your favorites—and then layer them on. More is more.

### COLORS
Bold. Turquoise, navy, green, red, pink, yellow, and white mixed with gold and silver metallics.

### ELEMENTS
Pattern, lacquer, Lucite, brass, wallpaper, bamboo, and mirrors.

### INFLUENCES
Old Hollywood. Kitsch. Vintage decorating magazines and coffee-table books. The big names of twentieth-century interior design: Dorothy Draper, Billy Baldwin, and David Hicks.

# warm industrial

Exposed brick, metal accents, and rustic details punctuate the usually loftlike space. Adding warmer, more comfortable textures and materials can make it work in any size room.

### COLORS
Darker neutrals, grays, blacks, browns, and navy, punctuated with a few powder-coated brights.

### ELEMENTS
Metal, rough-hewn wood, leather, canvas, copper, and glass; an aged patina is a definite plus.

### INFLUENCES
America's industrial past. True lofts. Vintage science lab equipment, old factory signage, and industrial antiques.

*continues* •••••••••➤

# style **DNA** (continued)

## new traditional

Classic formal design, relaxed and updated for how we
live today. Think familiar shapes in fresh colors.

### COLORS
Rich hues mixed with warm, creamy whites, deep
browns, and true blacks. Lighter and brighter accent
colors modernize the look.

### ELEMENTS
Dark wood tones, metals, marble, and gilt. Linen, wool,
and velvet fabrics. Stripes, plaids, and smaller-scale
patterns.

### INFLUENCES
Classic architecture and interior design. Family
heirlooms.

## simple chic

Beautifully (and thoughtfully) pared down. Individual
elements can range from rustic to luxurious, but the
overall palette is focused and elegant.

### COLORS
White, cream, pale gray, soft brown, black. Offbeat
pastels and clear brights as accents.

### ELEMENTS
Light or distressed wood, linen, cotton, felt, ceramic,
hand knits, glass, and pottery.

### INFLUENCES
French and Swedish country homes. Wabi-sabi. Shabby
chic.

## organic modern

An elegant balance between the minimal, clean lines of contemporary design and beautiful, often luxurious, natural elements and forms.

### COLORS
Clean neutrals with warm and cool whites—and other shades found in nature, like mossy greens.

### ELEMENTS
Raw-edge wood, leather, linen, silk, metallic finishes, marble, stone, and fur. Surface texture, simple geometric patterns, and plants.

### INFLUENCES
Nature. Everyday luxuries, like the perfect teapot or wool blanket. Japanese interiors. Contemporary furniture design.

## contemporary cottage

Casual yet chic. Comfortable furniture in welcoming rooms that convey a strong sense of style without sacrificing homey warmth.

### COLORS
Creamy whites, denim blues, rosy reds, mustard, and olive.

### ELEMENTS
Warm woods, canvas, wool, enameled metals, milk-painted wood, and soft lighting.

### INFLUENCES
Cottages and country homes. British B&Bs. Seaside getaways.

# 4

# color

Color is a direct reflection of personality.

You want to choose a palette that makes you feel happy in every room. Because it is so personal, though, picking the right shade can be a real stumbling block; it's easy to hesitate and not express yourself fully.

But we say . . . go for it!

The safest way to start thinking about color is to choose a palette from either the Warm Family (reds, yellows, oranges) or the Cool Family (blues, greens, purples). Picking a few shades within one of these two groups ensures harmony. As you get bolder, however, you can certainly start to mix warm and cool colors together: mossy green with canary yellow, crimson red with lapis blue . . . the options are limitless.

If you're a bit more adventurous with color—but still want some direction—get inspired by something you already own and love: a rug, a piece of artwork or clothing, even an element from nature, like an egg-shell, feather, or leaf. The fact that you love it means it will sing in your home—and the fact that all these colors already exist together means they'll work nicely in a room.

MAPLEWOOD, NJ
Mary + Lou Castelli
Mother + Private Equity Manager
daughter, Sienna + sons Colton, Rex, Bo

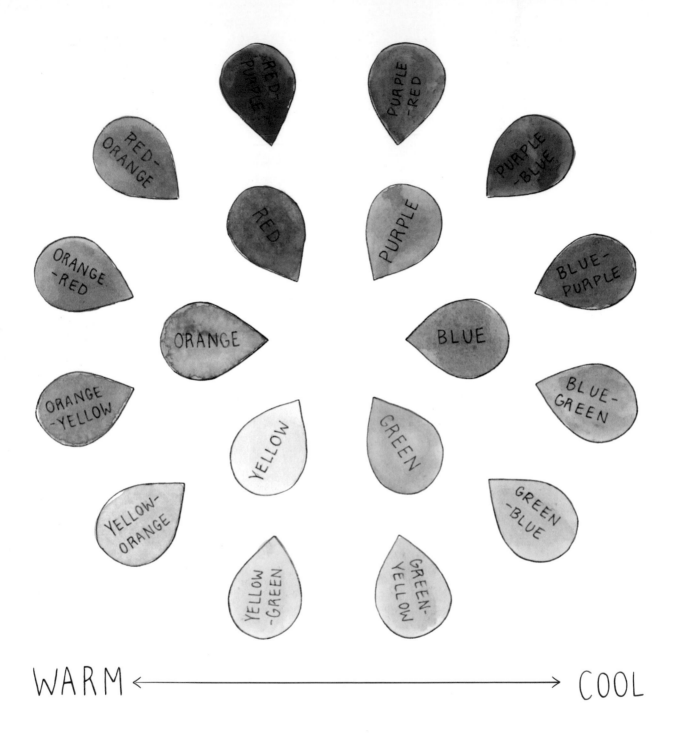

WARM ⟷ COOL

## taking the color splash

If you're ready for a bold mix, picking shades from opposite ends of the color wheel will always be complementary. Selecting hues that appear next to each other is a subtler combination that creates interesting definition in a space.

**THE 80/20 RULE** Before you get too color hungry, keep this in mind: a little bit of color goes a long way. Using whites, off-whites, and neutrals in up to 80 percent of a room, and then filling the other 20 percent with a highly saturated shade, gives you the right baseline mix. We call it the 80/20 Rule— and it's a sure guide to getting color right in every room. You'll find that once you start pushing color into your space, it will dramatically change the feeling of your whole home. But don't be timid; almost nothing is permanent when it comes to home decor . . . especially paint.

# color schemes . . . with a twist

We've designed one palette for each of our signature styles. Don't think of them as the only way to achieve these looks—think of them as a jumping-off point for making your own.

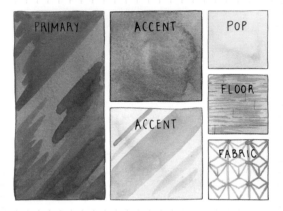

## warm industrial

**PRIMARY COLOR:** fern green
**ACCENT COLORS:** powder blue-gray + light silver
**ADVENTUROUS POP:** add marigold
**FLOORS:** medium-tone distressed wood
**FABRIC:** neon pink geometric print

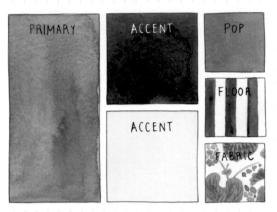

## happy modern

**PRIMARY COLOR:** azure blue
**ACCENT COLORS:** black + eggshell
**ADVENTUROUS POP:** add forest green
**FLOORS:** textured carpet
**FABRIC:** bold floral print

## simple chic

**PRIMARY COLOR:** dutch linen
**ACCENT COLORS:** soft pink + deep navy
**ADVENTUROUS POP:** add sunglow yellow
**FLOORS:** honey-tone wood
**FABRIC:** cowhide

## eclectic collector

**PRIMARY COLOR:** creamsicle orange
**ACCENT COLORS:** chalkboard + light yellow
**ADVENTUROUS POP:** add fuchsia
**FLOORS:** distressed cement
**FABRIC:** textured berber

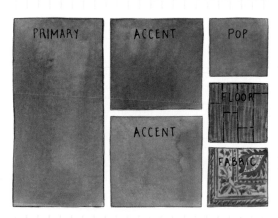

## classic glam

**PRIMARY COLOR:** gray

**ACCENT COLORS:** purple + olive

**ADVENTUROUS POP:** add tomato red

**FLOORS:** black wood

**FABRIC:** faded persian textile

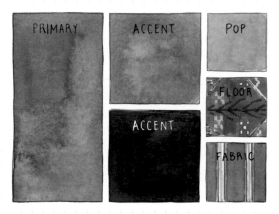

## contemporary cottage

**PRIMARY COLOR:** saddle suede

**ACCENT COLORS:** gray + ink

**ADVENTUROUS POP:** add kelly green

**FLOORS:** moroccan rug

**FABRIC:** rustic stripe

## organic modern

**PRIMARY COLOR:** white

**ACCENT COLORS:** pale gray + moss green

**ADVENTUROUS POP:** add silver

**FLOORS:** pale wood in herringbone pattern

**FABRIC:** french crochet

## new traditional

**PRIMARY COLOR:** subdued sea foam

**ACCENT COLORS:** chocolate + rich green

**ADVENTUROUS POP:** add ruby red

**FLOORS:** graphic patterned rug in a neutral shade

**FABRIC:** neutral check

**5**

# walls

Walls are one of the hardest-working elements in a home.

They define your floor plan, divvying up the footprint of your space into multiple rooms. Walls support artwork, bookshelves, coat hooks, mirrors, and lighting. And on top of all that heavy lifting, they play a key role in punctuating the design of your space.

Think of your walls as large canvases. With the right treatment, they can enhance light and color and greatly contract or expand a room. In fact, walls play just as much of a role in making your home feel big or small as its actual square footage.

While we've talked about flow as a function of furniture placement, good flow can also be established by alternating the colors of your walls from one room to the next. Bright walls reflect more light and have an expansive visual impact. Dark walls absorb light and feel closer to you visually. Put this lesson to use, and you have the opportunity to vary the experience in your home, from wall to wall to wall.

NEW YORK CITY
Michele Varian + Brad Roberts
Shop Owner, Michele Varian + Musician

# paint

Paint is much more than a decorative tool. You can use it to alter the perception of a room: make ceilings seem higher, walls longer, and open spaces cozier. Try these foolproof tricks when picking paint, and get the most from every wall in your house.

**BALANCE SOARING CEILINGS** If ceilings are so high that your room feels uncomfortably vast, consider painting them a darker shade. It gives the impression of closeness, which, in turn, is cozier.

**ADD HEIGHT TO LOW CEILINGS** White ceilings are what make most rooms feel higher than they actually are. You can increase the illusion, though, by adding a chair rail to your walls and painting the top half of the wall a lighter shade than the bottom.

**MAKE A SMALL ROOM FEEL LARGER** We've all heard that lighter colors help small rooms seem spacious. This is true, but an even more helpful trick is to paint your walls and ceiling the same color. It allows your eye to flow uninterrupted through the space, blurring the boundaries of the room.

**MAKE AN AWKWARDLY LONG SPACE MORE PROPORTIONATE** Painting the shorter "end" walls a few shades darker than the others can make a long, narrow space look slightly more square. Again, this is because the dark color creates the illusion of closeness.

**HIGHLIGHT (OR HIDE) ARCHITECTURAL DETAILS** Charming details like decorative molding should be showcased (when they're in good shape), so paint them a contrasting color to your walls. If, however, you want to hide eyesores (air-conditioning vents, radiators, exposed pipes), paint them the same color as your walls, and they'll blend right in.

# wallpaper

Wallpaper is a commitment. Putting it up is a lot of work. Taking it down is even harder. But as with all big commitments, you can expect big returns. Think of wallpaper as art on a very grand scale—and use these tips for choosing (and hanging) it wisely.

PAINT

## cheat sheet:
## common paint finishes, defined

**flat:** Matte finish; reflects minimal light. Great for bumpy walls, because it hides flaws. The downside: it marks easily, so only use it in low-traffic areas.

**eggshell:** Semimatte finish with a very subtle sheen. The best option if you want the look of flat paint but need something more durable that can be cleaned—for, say, a dining room.

**satin:** A smooth and slightly glossy finish. Good for walls in high-traffic areas, such as living rooms, because it wipes clean without damaging the paint.

**semigloss:** Glossy without being shiny. It's highly durable, making it the right choice for bathrooms and trim, which take a lot of abuse.

**gloss:** High-shine and ultradurable. It stands up to grease and water stains, which means it's great for kitchens, doors, and attention-grabbing pops of color. One drawback: it shows every bump and flaw in the wall.

WALLPAPER

**LARGE PRINTS** Busy or oversize prints sing in small rooms (bathrooms, entryways) or on one statement wall in a bigger space (above a fireplace, behind a media center). If you've decided to use a large-scale print, then make this the starting point of your design vision, and build the rest of the room's decor and color scheme around it.

**SMALL PRINTS** Almost any room can handle a smaller print. Use it to offset a stronger pattern in something you already own, like a rug or piece of furniture. Or hang it as a way to highlight an architectural detail (a kitchen nook or arched ceiling).

**REMOVABLE WALLPAPER** Loads of big-name companies and new designers (Tempaper, for instance) offer hundreds of design options. If you're renting (or a commitment-phobe), removable wallpaper is the perfect solution. With a little elbow grease, it pulls right off the wall when you're ready to move—or when you get tired of it.

**PAINTING PATTERNS** If you like the idea of pattern on your walls but don't want to spend the money on wallpaper, you can always create your own design using painter's tape and paint. Taping off the pattern is time-consuming. But the added bonus of having something totally unique (that you made) in your home is immeasurable.

## tile

Decorative Turkish, Moroccan, and Mexican tiles have changed the game when it comes to tile and where it's used in the home. Once reserved for bathrooms and kitchens, decorative tile work is now popping up on statement walls in living rooms and outdoor spaces. As with wallpaper, the commitment level is high, but the payoff is big. A good compromise: tile a small area first, then add more if you decide you love it.

TILE

# Floors, like walls, provide a huge visual impact in a room.

Because they live beneath your feet, however, you experience them more unconsciously—so it's easy to overlook them when thinking about style. Don't let this happen to you.

# floors

Consider the floor your fifth wall. How you choose to treat it can make a room feel bigger or smaller, warmer or cooler, and the acoustics louder or softer. With all those elements at stake, it's a good idea to design a space from the floor up, selecting a material (hardwood, cement, carpet, tile, and so forth) if you can, then layering on a rug or two.

Start the decision-making process by looking at the interplay between your floor and walls. No matter which material you select (flip the page for help sifting through the many options), the most common combination—and the one we'd recommend—is having floors that are darker than your walls. This grounds the space, while extending the walls upward visually. If, however, your walls are a dark color, you may want to opt for lighter floors that will help brighten the room. For the most part, it's wise to avoid matching the two surfaces: dark-on-dark feels cavelike, while light-on-light lacks definition.

In addition to achieving flattering color coordination, a room also needs softness and warmth—which you get by adding rugs and carpets. As a good rule of thumb, we prefer carpets in bedrooms and closets (where it can absorb a great deal of sound), and we like rugs (the more decorative option) everywhere else. Our advice: Get your floors into good shape, then cover them with lovely rugs to make your home cozy and beautiful.

LOS ANGELES
Anne Ziegler + Scott Mason
Trend Forecaster + Entertainment Executive

## YOUR need to know

# flooring

## hardwood

One of the oldest types of flooring—and currently the most popular. Hardwood can be used throughout your home, though we'd recommend going with something more water-resistant, such as tile, in bathrooms and kitchens.

**WHAT'S TO LOVE:**

• Hardwood floors make a space feel "high end."

• Easy to clean and very durable (hardwood can last hundreds of years).

• Add value to your home.

**WHAT YOU SHOULD KNOW:**

• Depending on the type of wood and finish you choose, hardwood can be expensive. (Macassar Ebony, for instance, is $150 per square foot!)

• Noise is an issue, especially with pets. The clicking of their nails can slowly drive you crazy.

• You can't hide scratches or dents (though some people prefer a weathered look).

## laminate

Not your granny's kitchen floor. A lot of laminate today is engineered to look like hardwood or tile, with many of the benefits and almost none of the problems. It can be used in every room of the house.

**WHAT'S TO LOVE:**

• Much less expensive than traditional hardwood or tile.

• It's more resistant to scratches and dings.

• Sound doesn't echo quite as much.

**WHAT YOU SHOULD KNOW:**

• Even the best laminate will have a slight sheen. Discerning friends will know it's not the real thing.

• The feel is not quite as solid underfoot as hardwood or tile.

• Some laminates are vulnerable to spills. Liquids can cause rippling and buckling if not cleaned up quickly.

## ceramic tile

Most commonly used in high-traffic areas, such as kitchens and bathrooms. The options are varied: porcelain or non-porcelain, glazed or unglazed. In general, non-porcelain is cheaper, but porcelain is more durable and naturally stain-resistant.

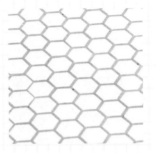

**WHAT'S TO LOVE:**

• Ceramic tile is practically indestructible (unless you're prone to dropping anvils on your kitchen floor).

• Easy to clean.

• It's naturally germ-resistant, making it a great option in damp rooms.

**WHAT YOU SHOULD KNOW:**

• Ceramic tiles absorb heat, so they always feel cold.

• They're extra-hard (meaning, they're unkind to bare feet).

• Weight can be an issue with larger, thicker tiles. They can get heavy when covering a lot of square footage. Always have your subfloor and foundation checked before installing.

---

**a quick note on hardwood floor stains: light vs. dark**

**Light stains** look modern and help bounce light around the room. The downside: you'll see every speck of dirt that hits the ground.

**Dark stains** feel a bit more traditional, with the bonus of masking dirt. The downside: they can make a small room feel smaller.

## carpet

Usually reserved for areas you want to feel cozy or intimate, such as a bedroom or closet. There are dozens of materials to chose from—and equally as many piles (the length and shagginess of the carpet). Here are a couple basics to keep in mind: the longer the pile, the harder to clean; natural materials, like cotton, won't last long in high-traffic areas.

**WHAT'S TO LOVE:**
- There are a lot of really affordable carpeting options out there.
- Soft underfoot.
- Carpet (combined with its sub-padding) absorbs sound.

**WHAT YOU SHOULD KNOW:**
- It's hard to clean—and prone to stains and discoloration from the sun.
- Like clothing, it will absorb scent (both good and bad).
- Carpet ages quickly and will start to show signs of wear after 18 months.

## slate tile

Naturally dark and textured, this type of stone was once reserved for use outdoors, but it is now being installed in entryways, kitchens, fireplace surrounds, and bathrooms because of its extreme durability.

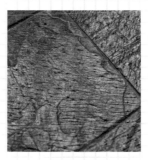

**WHAT'S TO LOVE:**
- Slate is an all-natural material with the warmth of wood and the endurance of tile.
- Waterproof and stain-resistant.
- It holds up beautifully in high-traffic zones.

**WHAT YOU SHOULD KNOW:**
- It can be pricey, especially when covering a large area.
- Tiles can crack under extreme pressure (furniture legs are a common offender).
- Again, since it is tile, it's cold—especially in winter.

## concrete

A fairly new choice in the flooring world, eco-friendly concrete is quickly gaining popularity for its low maintenance and versatility when it comes to finishes. It's great for those who want the same floors throughout their home, because it can be used anywhere.

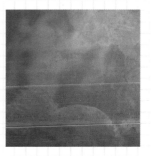

**WHAT'S TO LOVE:**
- There are multiple ways to finish concrete. It can be stained, dyed, painted, or left natural.
- Extremely affordable (depending how you choose to finish it).
- Lends itself to easy cleanup.

**WHAT YOU SHOULD KNOW:**
- Concrete will be cold—though it works well with radiant heating, if you're able to install it underneath.
- The end look of your floors can have a lot to do with how the foundation was poured or the finish applied—which you may or may not have control over. Getting a consistent look can be tricky.
- Concrete is heavy, so you'll need a strong subfloor and foundation to support it.

# the great
# rug layer-up

Large area rugs typically come with large price tags. Save some cash by layering a few smaller rugs together—just be sure that they complement one another. The key is contrast; the mix should look purposeful (not accidental). Here are a few of our favorite ways to achieve this.

layer rugs in the **same color palette**

layer rugs
of **different
textures**

layer rugs
of **different
sizes**

The right window treatments make the difference between a room that lures people in and one that feels a little off.

They can punctuate your style, hide architectural flaws, and control the overall light in a space.

When you're starting to think about window treatments, consider your needs. How much light control do you want? Is privacy a concern? What's the overall mood you're after: Cheery? Airy? Cozy? This helps limit your options (in a good way).

**For light control,** consider a mix of the following: sheer and opaque drapes, blackout curtains, louvered blinds, solar shades, shutters.

**For privacy,** consider the following: window films, top-down shades, cellular shades, woven shades, shutters.

**For mood,** consider the following: patterned curtains, Roman shades, extra-long drapes, colorful roller shades, modern rail systems, or creative solutions such as in-window shelving.

With function out of the way, you're freed up to think about style. Look at your window treatments as a combination of two elements: the light-controlling foundation and the interchangeable, decorative "outerwear." Then start doing your research. Pull inspiration from blogs, magazines, even Pinterest—keeping in mind the decor of the rest of your room. If you've used lots of patterns elsewhere, consider sticking with solid drapery, and vice versa. For curtains that "disappear" into the room, stay close to your wall color, but go a shade or two darker for definition. For added drama, turn up the color contrast.

The possibilities are endless, but once you've landed on a solid style direction, factor in cost and maintenance—then make a final decision. You never want to put off an opportunity to highlight your style while making a room feel "finished."

# 7

# windows

MILLBURN, NJ
Jessica + Scott Davis
Designer, Nest Studio + Marketing
son, Bryan + daughter, Lucy

# proper measurement is key

Whether you're making your own window treatments or ordering custom solutions, those that fit properly always look best. Don't cut corners: measure every window dimension to the nearest eighth inch—twice, even if they look identical. Here are a couple of tricks to help ensure you're getting a proper window measurement.

## curtains

**length** Determine where you want your rod to be mounted (4 inches above the window frame is standard), and start your measurement there—not from the top of the window. Be sure to adjust measurements to account for the hardware being used to hang your curtains: grommets, ties, curtain rings, etc.

For a standard, clean look, measure to the floor. If you want your curtains to break along the floorboard, add 2 inches. For a dramatic pooling of fabric, add between 5 and 8 inches.

**width** For a standard look, multiply the width of the window by 2. This should equal the width of a single curtain panel. For a more dramatic look, multiply the width by 3.

## shades + blinds

**inside mount** Clean and modern—and the best option if you're planning to layer treatments (since the entire shade or blind nestles neatly inside the window frame). It requires enough depth to accommodate the mounting hardware, usually 2 inches, but check your specific product. For width, measure the inside of your window frame at the top, middle, and bottom. Use the smallest measurement for your blind width. For length, add 5 inches to the height of your window.

**outside mount** More traditional but has the bonus of being a problem solver. It can make a window look larger or cover up imperfections. You need several inches of flat surface next to or above the window frame to install the mounting hardware. A standard width is 3 to 4 inches larger than that of your window (giving you an extra 1.5 to 2 inches on either side). For length, again, add 5 inches to the height of your window.

# shades + blinds

 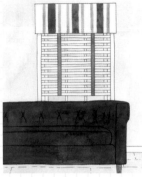  

## happy modern

**TYPE**
Roller shade.

**MOUNT**
Inside mount.

**MATERIAL**
A semisheer, heavyweight cotton in a bold, graphic pattern.

## new traditional

**TYPE**
Venetian wood blinds.

**MOUNT**
Inside mount.

**MATERIAL**
Wood blinds with a cotton tape ladder and matching fabric cornice.

## eclectic collector

**TYPE**
Tulip Roman shade.

**MOUNT**
Outside mount.

**MATERIAL**
Heavy, open-weave linen with a subtle stripe or texture.

## warm industrial

**TYPE**
Sheer, vertical solar panels.

**MOUNT**
Outside mount.

**MATERIAL**
An open weave in a neutral color. Keep in mind the sliding panels layer when opened and, therefore, look darker in color.

---

## *the* right curtain-blind combo

We've broken down the most common window coverings into easy-to-mimic treatments based on our eight signature styles. Feel free to mix, match, and reimagine them into something that's all your own.

## window film

In spots where privacy is a major concern—and curtains or blinds are out of the question—easy-to-use window films are the perfect solution. They diffuse light while blocking the view in both directions. There are hundreds of design options, from plain matte frost to a mixed-opacity faux stained glass.

# curtains

  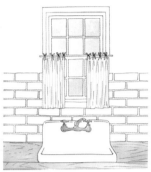

## classic glam

**HEADING**
Tiny pinch pleats, flowing into graceful, cascading volume.

**HARDWARE**
Curtain rings and a metal rod mounted 12 inches above the window frame to make a small window feel larger.

**DIMENSIONS**
Two panels, each the full width of the window. The length is nearly floor-to-ceiling to allow for 3 inches of pooling on the floor and a high-mounted rod.

**FABRIC + LINING**
Crinkled silk with heavy lining. Linen, damask, or velvet are also good options.

## organic modern

**HEADING**
Grommet with tailored pleats.

**HARDWARE**
A sturdy, brushed-metal rod mounted 4 inches above the window frame. *Note:* For a more organic-feeling finish, opt for wood mountings.

**DIMENSIONS**
Standard width. The length just touches the floor to keep the effect crisp and clean.

**FABRIC + LINING**
Lightweight cotton with no lining. Textured linen or canvas work, too.

## simple chic

**HEADING**
Rod pocket with pinch pleats.

**HARDWARE**
Keep it airy with a wooden rod and finials. Mount 2 inches from the top of the window frame to keep the pattern in check.

**DIMENSIONS**
Standard width (the less the fabric gathers, the more pattern you see). Allow 2 to 3 inches of pooling when measuring length, for a laid-back finish.

**FABRIC + LINING**
A bold color or graphic print on a sturdy cotton or canvas. Keep curtains from fading by lining them.

## contemporary cottage

**HEADING**
Café curtains with soft, inverted pleats.

**HARDWARE**
Curtain rings and a simple outside mount in brushed metal or wood.

**DIMENSIONS**
Standard width to allow for relaxed gathers. Height is approximately one-third to one-half of the full window height, hemmed to meet the bottom sill evenly.

**FABRIC**
Casual, easy-care cotton with no lining. A tonal stripe, medallion, or tiny floral print captures the mood perfectly.

Any great photographer will tell you that good lighting makes all the difference. The same is true in your home.

Lighting focuses your attention, makes colors deepen and shine, and adds a shimmering energy to a room.

While sunlight is best, you can't always control how much of it you get, so there are three other types of lighting to utilize. Each is important and should work harmoniously to create atmosphere and mood.

**Ambient lighting (or general lighting)** provides overall illumination and comes from pendants, chandeliers, ceiling lights, recessed lights, and wall-mounted fixtures.

**Work lighting** is bright, focused light in areas where you read, cook, or get ready in the morning. It typically comes from desk lamps, floor lamps, track lighting, and vanity lights.

**Accent (or focal) lighting** creates visual interest and draws attention to the parts of your home you want to showcase, like artwork or architectural details. It often comes from track lights, indoor spotlights, recessed lights, or picture lights.

Using just one of these light sources, no matter how bright, will never make a room feel comfortable. The most visually interesting spaces have multiple points of light (at least three) that work together to create an overall glow. When starting to think about lighting schemes in your home, keep these steps in mind.

1. Start with work lighting. Consider the functionality of your space, and add work lighting in areas that need it.
2. Feather in accent lighting to highlight your favorite areas: a mantel or art wall, for instance.
3. Take stock of the current lighting situation; then fill in with ambient light.

# 8

# lighting

NEW YORK CITY
Maxwell Ryan
Apartment Therapy Founder
daughter, Ursula

# light sources, defined

### pendants + chandeliers

Think of them as the jewelry of your home. They add drama and personality and quickly update a room—especially for renters who may feel stuck with ugly overhead fixtures. Try one of these lighting scenarios in your space, and be prepared for immediate (and effective) results.

- **Mount one over a dinner table to create an inviting or romantic atmosphere.**
- **Hang a row of pendant lights to visually separate an open floor plan.**
- **Punctuate a sitting area in a bedroom or living room by adding a low-hanging fixture.**

### table lamps

Lamps are one of the most fun ways to put your design stamp on a room. Where it gets tricky, though, is selecting the correct size. A table lamp should be proportionate to the furniture it sits on. That means the shade should be no larger than one-third of the table's surface. And it should be tall enough to provide light without shining directly into your eyes. A good rule of thumb: make sure the bottom of the shade is at eye level when you're sitting next to the lamp on a sofa, chair, or upright in bed.

### track lighting

The ultimate multitasker, track lighting (a line of lights attached to a rail on the ceiling) has the ability to fill the role of ambient, task, and accent lighting all at the same time. Directing individual lights toward the ceiling creates ambient lighting. Angling them at specific elements, such as artwork, turns them into accent lighting. And if you rotate them toward a kitchen island or desk, they become task lighting. You get the flexibility of creating custom lighting schemes with one system. In other words: if you're looking for easy, you found it.

## table lamps: the just-right fit

TOO BIG

TOO SMALL

JUST RIGHT

# let's talk bulbs

Traditional incandescent bulbs are being phased out in favor of energy-efficient options. Here's what you need to know about the three main types of bulbs taking their place.

 **CFL (compact fluorescent light):** They last ten times longer than an incandescent bulb and produce less heat. Some CFLs can be dimmed, but not all. *Note:* They contain small amounts of mercury and should be recycled properly.

 **LED (light-emitting diode):** One of the most energy-efficient options. Expensive in comparison but cheap when you factor in their life span—typically up to 25 years. Most LEDs work with dimmers.

 **Halogen Incandescents:** The closest in resemblance to incandescent bulbs in light quality and shape. However, they aren't as energy-efficient or as long-lasting as the other options. Can be used with dimmers.

## cheat sheet: watts to lumens

New energy-efficient bulbs come with a new way of measuring light. Instead of how much energy a bulb consumes (wattage), measurements are now based on how much light a bulb puts out (lumens). This quick guide will help you understand the conversion.

LUMENS

# A home without art is not finished.

**9**

## art

Artwork, whether a drawing, photograph, poster, or careful stack of polished stones on a windowsill, is both wonderfully impractical and deeply important at the same time. With art, you express your true self, lifting your spirit up out of the material crush of your daily life. In this way, the things that matter most to you should be on prominent display. Nothing can inspire instant happiness like opening the front door to a painting that makes you smile.

Beyond its role in self-expression, art goes hand in hand with decor. It can be used to inject color or express a mood, and, what's more, it's usually mobile. Artwork can—and should—be moved around often to continuously shift how you feel in a space. Hang a statement work alone, group things together like puzzle pieces across a wall, or keep the mood easy by propping frames on a ledge or atop a stack of books.

If you haven't started your art collection (however you choose to define it), now is the time to get inspired. A well-curated assortment adds heaps of personality to a home—and can become your most valuable possession. Most objects can be replaced; art rarely can.

CHICAGO
Brenda + David Bergen
Graphic Designer + Digital Media Consultant
son, Daniel

# art

## . . . as a single focal point

If you have one piece of spectacular art that's your pride and joy, or that is particularly large, place it on a prominent wall or surface. Use it as a jumping-off point for decorating decisions in the rest of the room—or keep the space minimal, and let the art shine.

## . . . as a gallery wall

Display a number of smaller art pieces together to cover more space—and make a bigger impact. This is one of our favorite decor trends of the moment. But the downside is . . . gallery walls can be tricky to get right. Spacing is your big-

gest ally: leave 3 to 6 inches of empty wall space between each piece (and keep whatever distance you choose consistent). Avoid the temptation to fill a wall by placing frames farther apart. The goal is to create a cohesive unit, not a scattered mess. With this in mind, there are three ways to organize your gallery wall.

**even rows**  A folio series (art with related subject matter) is strongest when hung in matching, thin frames and stacked in neat rows—either vertically or horizontally.

**symmetrical composite** If you have art that varies in size and shape, you can still arrange it in a symmetrical pattern. Create a grouping with clean, even borders, where the art is "contained" inside an imaginary rectangle or square. Just make sure to stagger art of the same size, so you don't end up with too many similar pieces in a row.

**asymmetrical** This arrangement mixes colors, textures, and styles—and feels more eclectic and personal as a result. Balance is key, though. Start with your largest piece as an anchor; then offset it with smaller frames and objects, hanging items at equal increments beside and above your anchor. Stick with similar frame styles or colors to keep things from looking too chaotic.

## . . . as decorative objects

Not all art fits into a conventional frame. Some of the most exciting collections integrate dishes, taxidermy, pottery, and other objects into gallery walls or grouped vignettes on tabletops or other flat surfaces. In this case, too, each object is less significant than the greater whole. Arrange items in groups of odd numbers (threes or fives are nice) and varying heights.

# how's it hanging?

Save your walls from being riddled with holes; check out this guide to hanging art before breaking out the hammer and nails.

1 **Don't hang it too high.** Most galleries hang art 57 to 60 inches on center (that's the measurement from the floor to the center of the piece of art). With groupings, think of the collective as one big element, and apply the same principle.

2 **Adjust for seating.** In dining rooms or offices, where people are primarily seated, it makes sense to lower art slightly to about 48 inches.

3 **Allow for headroom.** When mounting over furniture, keep 3 to 6 inches of wall space above a sofa or headboard; 4 to 8 inches above a table. This is close enough to keep the two elements visually connected but far enough that you won't bang your head when sitting and standing.

# let's talk frames

The art will steer you to the right frame if you let it. Choose a style and color that complements the piece and its surroundings.

## picking a frame

As a general rule, use a thick frame for large art and a thin frame for small art. The variety of styles (both store-bought and custom) is huge, but most fall into these categories:

**modern** Sleek metal or wood frames—usually with a thin profile—and a white mat; great with high-contrast art.

**transitional** Understated frames (with little ornamentation) and a neutral mat. Complements most styles of art.

**traditional** Typically more ornate, with a wider profile. Often warm wood or brass, this style works well with representational (versus abstract) art.

## picking a mat

As art gets larger, so should the width of your mat. This allows your artwork room to "breathe" and be noticed. In most instances, when it comes to color, choose a mat that's lighter than the art but darker than the wall it hangs on. Neutrals are best, so when in doubt, stick with white or off-white.

## frame alternatives

If spending loads of cash on framing isn't in the budget, get creative. You can use washi tape to casually stick prints to the wall (opposite). It's delicate enough to be pulled off without damaging your art. Or try covering your art with a sheet of clear acrylic and securing it in place with four L-hooks (also known as square-bend hooks). The result is minimalist and chic (and cheap!).

### unexpected art

Elevate everyday objects by hanging them, like art, on a wall. (Bonus: it might save you some storage space.)

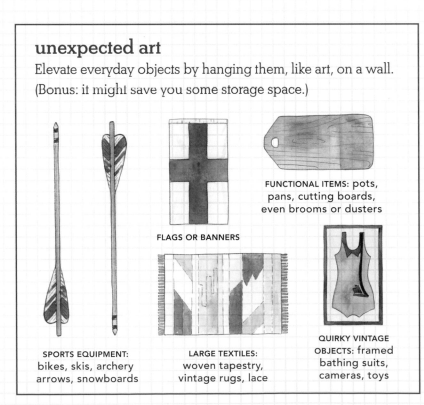

**FLAGS OR BANNERS**

**FUNCTIONAL ITEMS:** pots, pans, cutting boards, even brooms or dusters

**SPORTS EQUIPMENT:** bikes, skis, archery arrows, snowboards

**LARGE TEXTILES:** woven tapestry, vintage rugs, lace

**QUIRKY VINTAGE OBJECTS:** framed bathing suits, cameras, toys

If you've got style, you have fresh flowers in your home.

# 10

# plants

If you've really got style, you have cool plants growing inside and out. Heck, if you're superstylish, there might even be a tree growing in your living room.

Plants can be one of the most challenging things to keep up with at home, but the benefits far outmeasure the time commitment. Growing things brings out your nurturing side, whether it's a single succulent in your kitchen window or a whole garden in your backyard. Plants add clean air and healthy humidity and contribute fascinating and intricate organic shapes and colors to your landscape.

On Apartment Therapy, we've written for years about the pleasures of caring for plants. Here, we're condensing it all down to the essentials. The homes you see throughout this book range from warm climates to cold ones, but each owner has found a way to live with plants. In states like California they surround themselves, inside and out, with remarkable shapes and colors year-round. In the Northeast, they look forward to letting their yard go crazy in spring, while taking satisfaction from the small houseplants they nurture through the colder months.

It boils down to one simple lesson: something leafy and green and happily growing is the sign of a home that's truly alive and cared for.

LOS ANGELES
Judy Kameon + Erik Otsea
Landscape Designer + Outdoor Furniture Designer
son, Ian

# 5 (semi-) indestructible houseplants

## tillandsia (air plants)

**LIGHT:** Bright, indirect light is best.

**WATER:** Soak in water for 20 minutes per week, or mist lightly more often.

**MAINTENANCE:** These require no soil to grow. However, they won't survive in frost, so keep them away from windows come winter.

**SPACE:** Each tillandsia will bloom once in its life (midwinter to midsummer, depending on the species) but only grows a few inches per year.

**EXTRAS:** Because they draw moisture from the atmosphere, make sure your tillandsia vessel allows plenty of air circulation.

## jade tree

**LIGHT:** Moderate; several hours of indirect light per day is ideal.

**WATER:** Once every two weeks; allow the soil to dry completely between waterings.

**MAINTENANCE:** Little. Prune dead leaves intermittently; repot when necessary (usually every two years).

**SPACE:** Jade trees can easily grow up to 4 feet in height and width.

**EXTRAS:** You can mold the shape of a jade tree by pruning it in spring or early summer, when the plant is actively growing.

## cast-iron plant

**LIGHT:** Filtered light (or even shade) is ideal. Avoid full sun.

**WATER:** Does best with consistently moist (but not soaking wet) soil.

**MAINTENANCE:** This plant isn't picky about soil conditions or fertilization but should be repotted every other year.

**SPACE:** They typically grow to be between 12 and 15 inches in height and width.

**EXTRAS:** Cast-iron plants also make excellent outdoor ground cover. Just be sure to space them 1 to 1.5 feet apart to allow for growth.

## cyclamen

**LIGHT:** Bright, indirect light is best.

**WATER:** Only when soil is dry, about once a week. Avoid wetting the leaves or blooms.

**MAINTENANCE:** When the blooms die in summer, the plant is in a resting phase. Move it to a cool place until the next season, when this perennial will bloom again.

**SPACE:** Most cyclamen are happy in a small to medium-size pot.

**EXTRAS:** Cyclamen bloom in cool weather, so they're a perfect, leafy complement to most other flowering plants that blossom in summer.

## rosemary

**LIGHT:** Full sun.

**WATER:** Let soil dry between waterings, and make sure the pot has enough drainage to prevent rot.

**MAINTENANCE:** Rosemary doesn't like temperatures below 30 degrees, so keep it away from windows in winter.

**SPACE:** Unchecked, a rosemary plant can reach up to 3 feet but can also be easily pruned to accommodate a smaller space.

**EXTRAS:** A young rosemary plant takes time to get started, so don't expect major growth in the first twelve months. Year two is when this herb really gets going.

# OUTDOOR GARDENS what to consider before planting a thing . . .

### HOW MUCH GRASS DO YOU WANT TO MOW?

Come spring and summer, having a lawn means racking up some major mower mileage. If you can dedicate the time to maintaining it, divvy up your outdoor space with lots of grassy areas (a plus if you have children who need a place to play). If, however, the upkeep feels like too big a commitment, consider creating easy-to-maintain islands (well-defined areas with a specific type of ground cover, like pine straw, moss, or bark).

### HOW MANICURED DO YOU WANT YOUR GARDENS?

The symmetry of a manicured garden requires constant upkeep. (It's not in a shrub's nature to grow in a perfect square!) The visual beauty of a yard well kept, however, can only by outshined by your own sense of gratification in your accomplishment. Our advice: start small and build slowly, adding new beds as you get more comfortable with the amount of work it takes to care for what you've already planted.

### WHAT PLANTS WILL THRIVE IN YOUR YARD?

Don't make a beeline for every pretty flower at your local nursery. The truth is, though beautiful, they may or may not be compatible with your yard's soil and light. Instead, start with some research. Check out what's growing in your neighbors' yards. Have your soil tested, so you know what type of plants will work well for you. And, if you have pets, double-check that what you want to plant isn't harmful to them (some plants are poisonous).

### DO YOU WANT TO EAT WHAT YOU GROW?

If you have the space, growing herbs, veggies, or fruits is a supersatisfying way to get the most out of your yard. These days, people are planting cauliflower, kale, cabbage, and the like in their regular gardens not only for consumption but also because of their colorful foliage. One note of caution: city residents should test their soil for contaminants before growing edibles. If your soil proves unfit, build a self-contained bed with a liner and new soil.

### WHAT'S THE 12-MONTH PLAN?

It's easy to get carried away with planting in spring and summer. With all the gorgeous flowers in full bloom, you just want to inject as much color as possible into your yard. But planting with only one season in mind means your yard is bare the rest of the year. It's a much better idea to think in blooming cycles, picking a handful of plants and flowers that will thrive in each of the four seasons. This guarantees that there's always something new and interesting popping up.

# the no-lawn garden

No lawn? No problem. Consider one of these small-space alternatives.

## vertical garden

Going vertical means lots of plant real estate in a very small footprint. Hanging systems can use an existing fence or railing, or, if you have a little more space, a vertical planter, shelving, or trellis will give you plenty of decorative and organizational options.

## container garden

Great for decks, patios, or balconies of any size. Small plants live in portable vessels (on their own or creatively grouped) so they can easily move into sunny spots or indoors if it gets chilly.

## upside-down garden

Who says your garden needs to be right-side up? Common for tomatoes or herbs, inverted planters are clever contraptions that allow your plant to grow while hanging upside down.

MAPLEWOOD, NJ
Mary + Lou Castelli
Mother + Private Equity Manager
daughter, Sienna + sons Colton, Rex, Bo

PART TWO

# living in
# your home

**11**

# entryways

**HOOK. LINE. SINKER.** (LEFT)
A series of wall-mounted hooks
are a good-looking way to
customize storage in an entry.
Just obey the cardinal rule: one
item per hook, or your wall could
start to resemble a messy closet.

**POP ART.** (OPPOSITE) A grid of
black-and-white posters are hung
in bright, cherry-red frames. The
unexpected color choice turns
what could have been a plain-
Jane display into something far
more special.

# the southwest-gone-bright entry

One of the bonuses of living in an older home in Austin (such as this one
from 1905) is that a dedicated entry hall is quite often part of the deal.
Not always so generously sized in modern houses, this kind of space
provides a golden opportunity to set the style story of your home and
make organization a priority from the moment you cross the threshold.

This bright, spacious entry does a great job of disguising its smart
function in fun, pop-y, Southwest decor. Striped wall hooks, in a trio
of different sizes, serve as a semipermanent home for daily-use items,
like winter scarves or a favorite bag. The extra-long, rustic bench, a flea
market find, is a more temporary drop zone and place for things you
don't want to forget in your morning rush. An easy-to-clean cotton rug
protects the wood floors in such a high-traffic zone, while also waking
up the whole space with its traditional Southwestern pattern and
modern-bright color scheme.

AUSTIN
Sara Oswalt
Fashion/Interior Stylist

**A COLLECTOR'S EYE.** (LEFT) The beautiful red pom "flowers" are actually mini antique dusters the homeowners upturned at a local vintage store—proof that beauty can be found in the most common objects.

**PERSONAL GREETING.** (OPPOSITE) This couple takes turns rotating in photographs and mementos, such as the dried roses, for a sweet "welcome home" surprise.

# the "quick" entry

This glowing entryway greets you when you arrive on the thirtieth floor of a Brooklyn high-rise. Part streamlined function and part personal whimsy, it takes care of business *and* lifts your spirits as soon as you open the door.

If your home is a footwear-free zone—like this one—a bench makes kicking off and slipping on shoes simple, an ease that's extra-important when you have a large dog that loves walks. And since this space is more of a long hallway than a spacious mudroom, wall-hung storage plays a huge role in keeping the chaotic comings and goings flowing smoothly.

Even the practical components of this entryway set the right, welcoming tone. The artwork and photographs propped on the bench are a nice way to signal a return to a private, personal space. The red pom "flower" is purposely placed to the right of the entryway, farther down the hall. The flash of color not only catches your attention, but red, according to feng shui, draws good energy and luck through your doorway.

BROOKLYN
Moon Rhee + Heyja Do
Shop Owners, Dear: Rivington+

# the indoor/outdoor mudroom

Nestled in the steep hills of Laurel Canyon, this 1930s home greets its guests with a tangle of greenery that follows them up the stairs and flourishes at the front door. There, they'll find an entryway in two parts: the bit that's inside and the bit that's out.

Not every home has space inside its doorway for a bench. Here, the homeowners rather smartly expanded their usable space by placing an industrial metal bench outside the glass front door, which is usually left open. This means all the "shoe business" (taking them off, putting them on) doesn't need to happen within the tight quarters of the actual entryway.

Inside the small mudroom, the pine floors are lightly whitewashed, and everything else is painted a flat white. This combination brightens the space while providing a great backdrop for a unique collection of plants and art. The cerulean blue chair, coat closet, and rustic table are there for function—dropping off keys, hanging up jackets. But the most stunning piece of all is the immense ceramic bowl; its surprising contrast to the small objects around it catches your eye from almost every other room of the house.

**BEVY OF BEAUTIES.** (LEFT) As with art and collections, plants look great in multiples. Scattered at the front door in mismatched pots, this makeshift "garden" is far more interesting than a single planter.

**SURPRISING SCALE.** (RIGHT) This huge ceramic bowl sits under a tiny John Derian print. The play between big and small is a fun variation on the norm.

**FEET FIRST.** (OPPOSITE) No front door is complete without a good door mat. Sure it will keep shoes clean, but, really, it is an opportunity to add more color and texture to your entry.

LOS ANGELES
Anne Ziegler + Scott Mason
Trend Forecaster +
Entertainment Executive

**LINE 'EM UP.** (LEFT) Watches and eyeglasses are stored on the entryway table so they're not forgotten on the way out the door, while change bowls are set up as an organized way to empty pockets at the end of the day.

**ENDLESS RUN.** (OPPOSITE) The slimmest member of the rug family, a runner is a great (typically affordable) way to inject a hallway with style. If you have the length, play around with layering different colors or patterns.

# the never-too-thin entry

Even when space is tight, there's always an opportunity to carve out an entryway moment that makes your life easier. The narrow hallway of this newly renovated apartment in SoHo is proof of that. It takes full advantage of wall space as you move from the front door to the dining room, sprinkling strategic storage moments along the way.

Every piece was thoughtfully selected to serve a purpose. The half-moon entry table has no sharp edges—a danger in tight quarters on chaotic mornings—and serves as a landing strip where bowls of change and watches are lined up and waiting. For last-minute tie checks, a mirror was placed just inside the door. And in the distance, an Eames hanging rack catches all the winter coats and hats.

But this hardworking space isn't all function. Entryways also make excellent gallery walls for art. The cluster of photos and cutting boards here fill the space and make the hallway feel more crowded, but this is intentional. Beyond this narrow passage, the walls open into white expanses. The contrast between tight-and-cozy and bright-and-airy packs a visual—and very memorable—punch.

NEW YORK CITY
Maxwell Ryan
Apartment Therapy Founder
daughter, Ursula

**VINTAGE ACCENTS.** (LEFT) Labeling hooks in an entryway is helpful, but when done as thoughtfully as this, it can also become a decor boost. These were made using metal holders and printed labels that have all the charm of an old schoolhouse.

**GOOD GLOSS.** (OPPOSITE) Tough, higher gloss paint finishes are used throughout this home, which gives it a subtle but distinct European look. A bonus is how well this paint stands up to everyday wear and tear.

# the compact cottage mudroom

This clean and charming, small-space entry is like a breath of fresh air inside the home, the perfect spot to kick off your garden shoes after visiting the chicken coop in the yard, or to hang up your hat after a nice long walk with the dog.

This hardworking nook keeps things unfussy and practical. It mainly consists of hooks for keys, leashes, hats, and bike helmets and a compact bench, built for one—just the right size for pulling on rain boots (which, you'll notice, fit perfectly underneath) or stashing a bag of dry cleaning that's ready for drop-off. To help with flow through the tiny space—four doorways dead-end here—half doors were swapped in for full-size ones where possible.

Remember that not all entryways need to be supersized to be super-helpful. In this case, keeping the storage options minimal makes being organized easy. This space simply can't get overcrowded with stuff that doesn't belong, because there's only room for the things that do.

AUSTIN
Tim Cuppett + Marco Rini
Architect + Garden Designer

LOS ANGELES
Judy Kameon + Erik Otsea
Landscape Designer + Outdoor Furniture Designer
son, Ian

**12**

living
spaces

**MAGAZINE STAND.** (LEFT) Got a bunch of magazines you can't bear to part with? Sarah turned hers into a makeshift coffee table by creating two equal-size stacks of magazines (it works best if they're all the same title) and placing a piece of cut glass on top.

**ONE-OF-A-KIND FIND.** (OPPOSITE) This wooden lamp was found at a thrift shop. It's got beautiful, hand-carved bas-relief patterns and, as it turns out, was once a wallpaper-printing roller.

# the out-of-africa living room

Lots of entertaining happens here. It's the brightest and breeziest spot in the house, with high ceilings (11 feet) and a beyond-comfortable mix of versatile seating and classic, rich textures: well-worn leather, chrome, glass, and wood all float on a shaggy wool rug.

But the true star of this glowing space is the row of extra-tall windows that wrap the room on three sides. Outlined in beautiful Victorian window casings, these details could very easily have faded into the all-white walls. Painting the frames black, however (a project that can be done in a single Saturday afternoon), makes them pop against the very chic, very restrained, neutral palette in the rest of the space.

The furnishings are mostly vintage or secondhand, but the home-owner smartly chose these items in materials such as leather and chrome, which only get better with wear. A vintage springbok skin from Africa is layered over the armchair (instead of the floor) to heighten the pattern on that side of the room. And a DIY coffee table completes the look: a simple glass top supported by two stacks of vintage *W* magazines.

AUSTIN
Sara Oswalt
Fashion/Interior Stylist

**SEASONAL COLOR.** Yellow accessories and a pop of teal add a summery splash, but come winter they can be swapped out for something rustic and plaid to curl up in.

# the modern green den

Within this traditional suburban home beats a bright new modern heart. The four-story house was renovated a little at a time over an eight-year period with the help of interior designer Kristina Rinaldi. Each room is filled with upbeat energy and color while remaining open and spacious. Proof in point: this pop-y living room.

The first thing you spot, of course, is the supermodern green sofa. But the real surprise of this formal-looking room is how well it works for a family with four children under the age of six. There is plenty of play space, nothing to knock over, and all the furniture is easy to clean.

**GOOD EGGS.** (LEFT) Great rooms tell stories and here, two Egg Chairs, originally designed by Arne Jacobsen in 1958 for the Radisson Blu Royal Hotel in Germany, add a nice bit of design history.

MAPLEWOOD, NJ
Mary + Lou Castelli
Mother + Private Equity Manager
daughter, Sienna + sons Colton, Rex, Bo

**ONE BOLD THING. (CENTER)** This great Ruché sofa by Inga Sempé is the focal point of the room and shines among the calm, white surroundings.

**HUMOR WINS. (RIGHT)** When a room is serious about design, a little tongue-in-cheek humor takes the edge off. Designer Harry Allen's resin cast "piggy bank" is the perfect example.

Part of the delight of this room is how traditionally the untraditional furnishings are arranged. The sofa and chairs are centered on the fireplace, while the immense green rug defines the sitting area. Clean white walls (note the seamless transition between walls and ceiling) set off the spectrum of green, while black and gold accents add a graphic sharpness. A friendly ceramic pig holds court above the mantel (the perfect vantage point to take in all this bright fun), cementing this space as the happiest room in the house.

**RAW MATERIAL. (LEFT)** In very soft, upholstery-heavy environments, adding something raw and rustic, like this carved tree stump, as a counterpoint works really well.

**NEXT LEVEL RUG LAYERING. (OPPOSITE)** The patterns on the rugs get bolder as the rug's size gets smaller, so even with multiple colors and prints, this trio feels like one beautifully textural compilation.

# the dipped-in-gray living room

This cozy living room sits at one end of an old walk-up apartment. As in all railroad-style floor plans, the rooms are connected via one long hallway—and they, too, are long and supernarrow.

To balance the "bowling alley" flow, this homeowner played up the width of her living room (the apartment's widest point). The sofa is placed in front of the windows, with two soft chairs guarding the entrance, creating a lovely, meandering flow around the coffee table.

Adding to the perception of space is the design inspiration. The homeowner wanted the room to seem as if it were "dipped in gray." The painted walls were left bare, so light could reflect off them (a trick that makes the 11 x 13-foot space seem larger). And the gray notes continue around the room—a light shade on the sofa, darker on the chairs—with dots of gold and wood tones tossed in for warmth.

NEW YORK CITY
Emily Johnston
Photographer

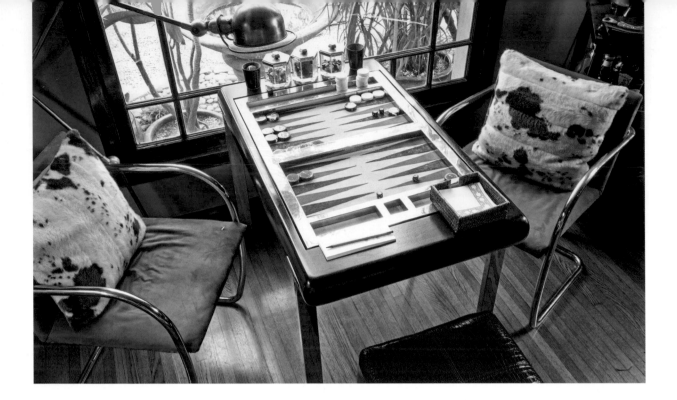

# the moroccan game den

Mixing warm and cool colors can be tricky to pull off, but this living room does it stunningly well. Deep bluish-green walls wrap the space, cooling the bright sunlight streaming through the windows. The dark color contracts the large area, making the walls appear closer (and the room cozier)—something you might not want to do in a smaller space with smaller windows.

The warm touches (tangerine chairs, canary yellow sofa, splashes of red in the accents) add to the coziness, while unifying the eclectic style: a little Moroccan, a little Spanish, and a little Art Deco with an endless supply of lovely small objects. The combination makes for a rich sanctuary that's unpretentious and instantly welcoming.

This is due in large part to the low-sitting, versatile furniture (you could plop down anywhere, even the floor, and be comfortable). Essentially, the room is divided into three parts: the game area, the gallery wall, and the fireplace—each with its own chairs, poufs, or stools. All the seating can come together to center on the immense coffee table and fireplace (for large parties), or it can split off into more intimate arrangements (for smaller gatherings). Clearly, this is a room for entertaining.

**BETTER THAN TELEVISION.** (ABOVE) Having a game constantly at the ready sends a very relaxed and inviting signal. In fact, a neighbor popped by to play a quick round of backgammon during our shoot.

**PHOTO-MAT IC.** (OPPOSITE) Typically, people hang dark frames on light walls; here your attention is grabbed by the reverse: black and white photographs surrounded by silver or black frames.

LOS ANGELES
**Lulu Powers + Stephen Danelian**
The Entertainologist + Founder, MeeLocal

**BLUE HORIZONS.** In a room so full of wonderful, rich design moments, it's smart to choose art that's not overly busy but still makes an impact.

# the soft traditional living room

At first glance, this living room may look traditional, but it isn't *really*. While the shapes fit that mold, the textural blend of the furniture and sunny pops of color are modern in every sense of the word.

Now, if you were to strip this room back to its bones, you'd have nothing but Sheetrock walls, cheap wood floors, and an echo-y large space. In other words, there are no architectural details to add character—all the soft warmth and welcoming comfort you see here are the result of strategically chosen (and laid out) decor.

**STACKED ICONS.** (LEFT)
Variations on the Apartment Therapy logo fill the corner of this room. The organic shapes and pops of color draw the eye up, emphasizing the tall walls.

**NEW YORK CITY**
Maxwell Ryan
Apartment Therapy Founder
daughter, Ursula

**OLD MEETS NEW. (CENTER)** This antique coffee table (a rescue that once belonged to Maxwell's grandmother) speaks of time gone by, something a room of mostly "new" furniture needs.

**AN ELEPHANT STOOD HERE. (RIGHT)** This Elephant Table, designed by Mark Sage, is modeled after those you see at the circus.

The large magenta rug defines the area, separating it visually from the open dining room it connects to. Two identically shaped sofas flank the rug: one in a soft white fabric, the other in contrasting dark velvet. Solar shades and white linen curtains filter the sunlight and improve the acoustics, and art finishes the space, drawing your attention up the high walls.

Balance is what really makes this glowing room come to life. The Ancient Greeks believed that a balanced room promoted good health. At the very least, it creates a calming and comforting—and visually cohesive—space.

**HARD LINES, SOFT FINISH.** Energy is created between the bright, white elements and the rich, dark ones. The movement between hard and soft, dark and light, color and neutral is what makes this room wonderful.

# the dramatically different country den

Inside this historic cottage sits a warm, masculine living room that will flip everything you've ever thought about country decor on its head. All the traditional hallmarks are here: plank walls, pine shutters, original light fixtures. And while these homeowners embraced the authentic details and country-cottage aesthetic, every other design choice brings this room racing from the 1850s into the present day.

The first thing you notice are the dark gray, high-gloss walls. They're not only dramatic; they serve a purpose. When the Texas temperatures start rising, this space is a cool respite from the heat. Likewise, come winter, the dark walls and wood-burning fireplace become a warm and cozy place to hide from the chill.

The eclectic seating (which reads like a history of handsome furniture) furthers the old-meets-new mix. Modern elements like the Florence Knoll sofa set off the more traditional choices in the room. When things start to get too match-y, they're intentionally mixed up. For instance, the leather armchair's footstool was re-covered in velvet to break up the pair. The result is a room that embraces the fact that its furnishings were collected over time.

AUSTIN
Tim Cuppett + Marco Rini
Architect + Garden Designer

**UNLIKELY INSPIRATIONS.** It's always smart to steal design notes from a favorite restaurant or bar. The idea to paint these walls such a deep, dark, glossy shade came from a small East Coast pub the homeowners once visited.

**GO FAUX.** (LEFT) Good decorating does not have to be fancy. Look closely: the green, marbled top on this vintage coffee table is not actually marble, but a cool, faux-painted rendition.

**FOCAL POINTS.** (OPPOSITE) Every room should have a "moment," big or small, that is eye-catching and special. Seen from the adjoining living room, this set of delicate green chairs demand your full attention in the study.

# the chinese-red retreat

This small jewel box of a room beckons you toward it—and doesn't want you to leave.

It is the work and home of interior designer Ruthie Sommers, who calls it "Ruthie on acid." The main focal points as you enter are a pair of lovely green chairs sitting in front of the bright French doors. But once you're inside, the corner banquette hugs the room, refocuses your attention on the coffee table, and envelops you in the rich, red moodiness of the space.

In truth, the room is awkwardly shaped, with a number of doorways and windows puncturing the walls. But you hardly notice all those architectural details, thanks to the offbeat but expert utilization of color. The use of one shade across the most prominent elements in the room (carpet, walls, banquette, trim, and doorways) draws your eye seamlessly around the space, so you take in the rich details without noticing every crevice in the wall.

While the color is intense (yes, that's a yellow lacquer ceiling), the quietness of the room is even more notable. The wall-to-wall carpet combines with the amazing, silk-upholstered walls to dampen the acoustics, increasing the intimacy and retreat-like feeling in this corner of the house.

LOS ANGELES
**Ruthie Sommers +
Luke McDonough**
Interior Designer + CEO, AirMedia
daughters Eloise, Bailey, Posey

**COLOR OVERHEAD.** While the whole room is exceptional, the true surprise is the yellow high-gloss ceiling. Most accent walls are actually walls, but for a real lift, painting the ceiling is a high-impact alternative.

# the fairy-tale living room

Take two steps into this whimsical living room, and you can't help but wonder if the Mad Hatter has taken up residence in a Chicago suburb. The dark formality and playful accents are so perfectly dreamlike, you immediately want to be submerged in this fairy-tale universe.

This room is cozy and stylish but also tough; everything is meant to be loved, used—and not worried about. (When you have four kids, that last part is very important.) Classic armchairs have been perked up with a clever upholstery solution—wool blankets—which wear well and are easy to clean. After a run-in with nail polish remover, the top of the coffee table was covered in a decoupage map (an "uh-oh" that turned into an "oh, wow"). And a Lucite trunk does double-duty as a side table and storage for the family's movie night blanket collection.

The practicality of the furnishings, however, doesn't sacrifice an ounce of dramatic style. As is the case with all great rooms, this one comes to life through its details. A statement wall covered in Orla Kiely wallpaper showcases a cherished painting. And an abundance of furry throws, paper streamers, and custom touches, like matching wallpaper-patterned lamp shades, add a splash of design magic everywhere you look.

**CUSTOMIZE IT.** (ABOVE) Plain white blinds wouldn't have been in keeping with this homeowner's stellar style standards, but these geometric ones most definitely are. When buying window treatments, forget basic and put your own stamp on it.

**PERSONALITY PEEKS.** (OPPOSITE) An absolute truth in decorating: always let a little bit of the real you shine through. This mom proudly lets her eccentric flag fly with giant antlers draped in a hot pink garland and a throw pillow shaped like a fawn.

BARRINGTON, IL
Michelle + Dave Kohanzo
CEO, Land of Nod + Banker
daughter, Emily +
sons Connor, Henry, Everett

# the scandinavian living room

Scandinavians love their clean-lined rooms and whitewashed floors that reflect light and keep interiors bright during the long, dark winter. Now, Los Angeles winters are neither long nor dark, but the pine floors you see here do bounce around a tremendous amount of sunlight. Pickled white and sealed with a pearl finish, the bare floors have a softly textured wood grain that shines.

The walls, too, are left a flat white, flowing right up to the gorgeous beamed ceiling. Within this glowing expanse, however, the home-owner has created a handful of simple, dramatic moments. Twisting wrought-iron ties are left black, illuminating this decorative element. A cerulean blue side table and vintage German botanical poster become a major statement, as do the armchair and scattered throw pillows covered in Josef Frank's remarkable fabric.

In a busier room, these small elements would disappear. But this space perfectly follows our 80/20 Rule (see chapter 4 for more on this), injecting just enough color to punctuate without overwhelming.

LOS ANGELES
Anne Ziegler + Scott Mason
Trend Forecaster + Entertainment Executive

**SCIENTIFIC EVIDENCE.** A vintage educational poster is just the bold statement these white walls need. Originally created in the fifties, sixties, and seventies, this poster (and others like it) are still being made by the same company today, Hagemann Wall Charts.

**FRANK FABRIC. (LEFT)** Anne is a huge Josef Frank fan. She inherited this love from her mother, who passed down two armchairs covered in Frank's cartoonish, remarkably colorful floral fabric.

**CURATED COLLECTIONS. (ABOVE)** All good collections hew to a common thread. Here, a gathering of Astier de Villatte ceramic bowls and bottles are pulled together by their glossy white finish.

living spaces **113**

# the hot & cold living room

The swirling sculpture floating across the back of this stunning room is not the largest piece of coral you've ever seen. It is, in fact, a fantastic use of Algue, modular pieces created by French designers Vitra Ronan and Erwan Bouroullec.

Hung with fishing line, the DIY art installation began as a simple grouping above the fireplace, but it has grown up and out to become a room-defining moment. The fluidity of the sculpture is balanced by the crisp geometry of the furniture in the rest of the space. Choices here lean toward modern classics, like the Womb Chair, but the bold embrace of color, from opposite ends of the spectrum, is where things get really interesting.

Mixing bright red and crisp navy in an all-white space runs the risk of coming off as a little "Fourth of July." That pitfall is avoided here thanks to a strategic separation of shades—red on one side of the room, blue on the other—and the addition of rich, textural components in shiny metallic and soft pink.

A contemporary space that's warm and welcoming is not easy to pull off; this mix of clean lines, cozy textures, and interesting visuals has the perfect yin and yang balance.

CHICAGO
Brenda + David Bergen
Graphic Designer + Digital Media Consultant
son, Daniel

**CAN'T BEAT THE REAL THING.** Initially, these homeowners purchased a (cheaper) replica of the classic Womb Chair but realized their mistake almost immediately (it was incredibly uncomfortable). There's a reason this particular chair has been coveted since 1948!

# the '70s living room

It takes skill to blend two decades' worth of design influences in one room—but, wow, can it pay off when you do.

This living room belongs to a jewelry designer and boutique owner, so the fashion dial has been turned way up. The historic 1930s bungalow is situated in Franklin Hills, and the architectural details are all hallmarks of the era when it was built: the intricate dark-wood trim, the detailed mantel, the elaborate window frames. But the furnishings tell the story of another decade.

Inspired by the '70s, plush armchairs topped with oversize furry pelts fill the room. A Lucite and glass coffee table adds sleekness while "disappearing" from view. And a rare Paul Evans credenza mirrors the fireplace on the opposite wall.

What brings it all together? Neutral brown tones that run through the wood, leather, and brass unify the space, while keeping the design eras from competing. Restraint also plays a big role. This furniture is large—there's a sofa just off camera, too—and the additional accents are minimal, ensuring that the decorative woodwork remains a focal point in this lush, old-meets-older living room.

**WOOLLY MAMMOTHS.** (ABOVE) Pelts made of wool are a great way to soften a room. These are seamlessly stitched together from smaller ones and super easy to find. (All of these were picked up on the cheap from Costco!)

**LET THERE BE MUSIC.** (OPPOSITE) This immense, burl wood credenza opens to reveal a curated record collection. The other side contains the turntable and digital stereo that connect to speakers throughout the house.

LOS ANGELES
Laura Jay Freedman
Shop Owner, Broken English

**ANALYZE YOUR SPACE.** This may seem like an unlikely spot for an armchair, but it was shimmied into the tight corner in order to take full advantage of the lush garden views it overlooks.

# 8 WAYS to supercharge your style

1 BE ABLE TO DESCRIBE WHAT YOU WANT . . . in words. When asked what you're looking for in a mate or career, the answers come easily. If asked about the style of a room, however, what you want can be harder to define. Having accurate words to convey your likes and dislikes is an important starting point. This extends beyond the things you put in the room (chairs, sofa, etc.) to how you want the room to feel.

2 DO YOUR RESEARCH. Scan decorating sites, magazines, and books, and pin or clip photos that appeal to you. Even if they're unrealistic for your space, you can get an idea of the colors, textures, and patterns you like. Finally, spend some time browsing stores to get a feel for what's out there—and what it costs.

3 CHANGE THINGS SEASONALLY. Style is not static. It's always shifting to reflect new experiences and interests—and your home should mimic that. At the beginning of every season, try putting away a few things. Then sprinkle a couple of fresh finds into the mix. They don't even need to be new! "Shop" from your bedroom for your living room—and vice versa.

4 ANALYZE YOUR SPACE. Spend some time sitting in different spots around your home to gain a new perspective on areas that might need work. Observe thoughtfully: Do you like the lighting from here? Is that space overcrowded? How would that art look with a wider mat and frame? Slowly making improvements will help you refine your style over time.

5 EMBRACE SAMPLES. Even the most confident decorator benefits from living with colors, patterns, or fabrics for a little while before pulling the trigger. Paint a few big squares on your wall, pin up wallpaper samples, and drape fabric swatches over furniture—then just let them be for a few weeks. Maybe you like them. Maybe you don't. But slowing down long enough to find out guarantees that you'll make better decisions.

6 THINK ABOUT SCALE. Envision a blank room. First, picture that room filled with a few large-scale pieces of furniture. Second, picture the room with more pieces of furniture that are smaller. Third, picture the room split evenly between the two: a few big pieces, a few smaller ones. Even without taking into account any other decorative elements, the first room you pictured will feel modern; the second, traditional; and the third, more eclectic.

7 TAKE PHOTOS. If you see something you like, snap a photo of it. Taking quick pics of design ideas as you encounter them is a great way to gather inspiration for future reference. Snap individual pieces or vignettes. Don't be shy about putting your camera phone to good use!

8 SHOP VINTAGE AND SECONDHAND. Sometimes it's easier to take a bigger style risk when an item is a one-off: a unique lamp at a thrift store or wildly printed pillows in a secondhand shop. Buying this way feels personal compared to encountering a wall of nearly identical pillows at a big-box store.

# eating spaces

# the french provençal dining room

Inspired by eighteenth- and nineteenth-century European homes, this sprawling—and perfectly divided—living room/dining room manages to feel both formal and incredibly welcoming.

The spare use of color, as well as the lack of curtains and absence of artwork, directs attention to the defining moments of this space: soaring 10-foot ceilings, antique pine floors in a point de Hongrie (herringbone) pattern, and triple-hung windows. There's power in the large-scale but simple nature of these elements. And in a room so full of built-in character, it's wise to select furnishings that blend into the setting, instead of trying to outshine it.

Everything from the rustic dining table to the mismatched antique garden chairs around it lends an inside-meets-outside feel to the space. Two large lemon trees create an "orangerie" along one side of the room in the colder months. But come spring, the trees are moved outside, and the windows are thrown open to their full height, turning them into multiple narrow doorways. Dining here is magical.

**SPRING GREEN.** (LEFT) Vintage Frette napkins with thick green stripes add just the right pop of color to this all-white tablescape.

**MEYER LEMONS.** (ABOVE) The bonus of having lemon trees in your living room is that you'll never lack a colorful centerpiece. The lemons in this bowl came straight from the trees.

**THE COOL DOWN.** (OPPOSITE) While this house was designed as a summer retreat, it doesn't have air conditioning. But thanks to the many large windows and carefully planted trees that block the sun, the whole home stays cool year-round.

EAST COAST
Deborah Nevins
Landscape Designer

STORAGE, STORAGE, EVERYWHERE. (LEFT) A window seat allows for maximum seating and storage. When it comes to the latter, think about what you're stashing. Jessica needed a place for cutting boards, so the cabinet openings are extra-wide.

FOLLOW THE LITTLE BLACK LINE. (OPPOSITE) Painting these French doors a crisp black pulls your eye straight to the corner retreat, creating a rich layer that (again) helps to visually separate the space.

# the breakfast nook

In even the tiniest space, it's possible to create a cozy dining area. You just need three things: nice light, a built-in window seat (or bench, if that's not possible), and a small round table.

To separate the tiny corner of this New Jersey kitchen into its own intimate room-within-a-room, it had to have a center and at least one element that helped to visually divide it from other spaces. This nook is centered on the window to the right, while the bench (loaded with hidden storage below) and large pendant light anchor everything. If you were to remove any one of these elements, this little room would begin to unravel.

Color completes this story. The homeowner hand-stenciled the finished-plywood floor to look like tile. The warm shades of gray are echoed on the walls and in the ikat bench cushion. For a pop of color (which is perfectly in line with our 80/20 Rule; see chapter 4 for more on this), bright pink and orange pillows line the window seat, offering a comfy spot for family breakfasts.

MILLBURN, NJ
Jessica + Scott Davis
Designer, Nest Studio +
Marketing
son, Bryan + daughter, Lucy

**DRINK-A-DOODLE-DO.** (LEFT)
These homeowners have a thing
for birds and taxidermy, so when
they spotted this rooster, it came
home with them immediately.
It now holds court over the
couple's small bar (and is the
official mascot of cocktail hour).

**PUT A PIN IN IT.** (OPPOSITE) Take
note of the pin-thin legs on this
dining room table. They balance
the fuller, more robust chairs
perfectly—so things don't feel
heavy in such a tight corner

# the glossy cabin dining room

Don't be fooled by the wood-paneled walls and mounted taxidermy;
this is not your typical rustic cabin in the woods. Hidden away on a
hilltop in New York's Hudson Valley, this open, modern, masculine
weekend home is an elevated version of everything you love about
escaping into nature.

Take, for instance, the glossy dining room. It sits in one corner of the
multipurpose living space (the kitchen, office, living room, and dining
area all exist in roughly 400 square feet). The layout is all function: it
squeezes neatly between the kitchen and the back deck, the table size is
perfect for intimate dinners for two, and the modern chairs tuck tightly
to the side of the table, conserving space.

But despite its pip-squeak size (and all that focus on functionality), it's
also a major style statement. The red lacquer table is all drama, while the
sleek drum pendant light grounds the space and adds its own particular
moodiness. The inside of the shade is covered in pebbled copper; turn
it on at night, and light flitters around the room like lightning bugs.
A taxidermy rooster and tabletop bar finish the space: a gorgeous
example of what can happen when rustic meets modern.

ELIZAVILLE, NY
Christopher Coleman +
Angel Sanchez
Interior Designer + Fashion Designer

# the farmhouse-in-a-skyscraper dining room

New furniture in a new-construction building can make for a particularly sterile room, no matter how amazing the view or great the location. Mixing in a few old things gives you depth and dimension. Mixing in all old things gives you a room like this.

Set in the thirtieth-floor penthouse of a brand-new tower in Brooklyn, this dining room has sweeping views from every direction. But even with the impressive Manhattan skyline as a backdrop, the focal point of this space is the 20-foot-long farm table. (The homeowners had to cut it in half lengthwise to get it inside.) Paired with an eclectic mix of chairs—no two are alike—the extra-thin table is both grand and intimate; the lack of width means you're always sitting close to one another.

While this open space could have been arranged into two or more individual areas with smaller furnishings, the unbroken length of the table creates a luxurious flow from the staircase to the living area, movement that's echoed by the stacked books and collected art at the base of the windows. If you have the means to do it, you can achieve grand results by letting a large space like this simply "breathe."

BROOKLYN
Moon Rhee + Heyja Do
Shop Owners, Dear: Rivington+

MIX WITH MEANING. Not necessarily intentional, this combination of a fig tree (earth), stacked books (mind), and African masks (spirit) shows the breadth of thought and feeling in this space. Comfortable rooms are aspirational as much as they are practical.

# the roundabout dining room

Located smack in the middle of a small Spanish bungalow, the dining room is the epicenter of this home. Every other room in the house is located off the sunny space, so passing through it is an almost hourly occurrence. To help with flow in this high-traffic zone, the smart home-owner picked a large round table and kept the rest of the furnishings minimal, which means there are fewer corners for energy to get "trapped."

With such a pared-down aesthetic, choosing big-impact pieces is important. At the center of it all is the amazing, 1930s dining table by Karl Springer (made from hundreds of pieces of inlaid bone). The twisting pedestal accentuates the table's roundness, a detail that's also echoed in the curved chairs by the same designer. A "halo" of lights punctuates the room—another standout vintage find, this one by Alvin Lustig—so even the lighting scheme has a circular gesture.

A graphic, oversize painting finishes the space. The piece was a cherished gift from a very good friend; a personal note that makes the whole room feel all the more special.

**SOME PEOPLE HAVE ALL THE LUCK!** (ABOVE) Karl Springer was a furniture designer in the seventies and eighties, famous for his use of exotic materials. Today, his work is hard—and expensive—to come by. Laura found these Springer chairs for a steal at the Rose Bowl Flea Market.

**MORE CURVES.** (OPPOSITE) Since most homes are filled with straight lines, the addition of curved architectural elements—like the arched doorways and built-in nook here—has a tremendous impact.

LOS ANGELES
**Laura Jay Freedman**
Shop Owner, Broken English

**DELICATE WHITES.** (LEFT) This stunning arrangement of white ceramic pieces forms the basis of a mobile tea set that's always at the ready.

**HIDDEN TREASURES.** (OPPOSITE) You never know what you'll find when you start renovating a hundred-year-old apartment. Michele discovered an old wedding photo, now hanging above the dining table, under the floorboards during construction.

# the dark menagerie dining room

This dark, gothic dining room may look as if it belongs in the country home of an eccentric French aunt, but it actually sits in a former factory space on one of Manhattan's busiest streets.

These homeowners eschew anything new or mass-produced in favor of vintage finds and artisan-made crafts. The wonderfully quirky blend keeps your eye racing around the open space in search of the next treasure. Framed gold mirrors by Brooklyn artist Ria Charisse hang next to vintage daguerreotype photographs and avian taxidermy. And the sweet oval table and leather banquette are set up just like a European brasserie, folding red café chairs and all.

But the true star is the Neisha Crosland wallpaper. Swirling floral shapes highlight the 12-foot ceiling while playing off all those dark wood frames. The wild pattern covers imperfections in the wall and transforms each surface into an artwork in itself.

The charm of this dark and cozy style is in its easygoing nature; this dining room is always ready for guests. As the homeowner says, "There's no reason to clean before a party; just make sure there's plenty to drink! Cleaning is for the day after."

NEW YORK CITY
**Michele Varian + Brad Roberts**
Shop Owner, Michele Varian + Musician

**DELICIOUS CONTRAST.** (LEFT)
We've always heard that food tastes better when it's served on round white plates. Whether you believe that or not, white plates are a classic that work well in a farmhouse setting.

**VINTAGE VESSELS.** (OPPOSITE)
When it comes to flowers, the rule in this house is that if it can hold water it can be used as a vase. Vintage jelly jars, water pitchers, antique medicine bottles—the options are endless.

# the country porch dining room

Everything in this sunny, window-lined room feels comfortably lived-in and well-loved, right down to the floor, which is made of hundred-year-old longleaf pine (once used as shelving at a local lumber yard).

By enclosing the original front porch, the homeowners were able to create this long, narrow dining room, grounded by a spectacular, equally long and narrow 10-foot dining table. The tabletop, which in a past life belonged to a carnival camp, sits on antique legs and is surrounded by a custom-made bench—the only "new" piece in the room—and a mix of collected-over-time, secondhand chairs.

A no-fail trick for helping to marry pieces of various styles and eras is utilized perfectly here: one coat of glossy, clean white paint, and the mismatched collection feels like a perfect set. Delicate, wire-frame café chairs provide a nice counterpoint to the sturdy wooden pieces, and they echo the pin-striped lines of the paneled walls. The light fixture, created from repurposed farm equipment, is intentionally left in its unfinished metal state to encourage more patina, adding to the lived-in look over time.

ROUND TOP, TEXAS
Paige + Smoot Hull
Bed & Breakfast Owners
son, Pierce + daughters Eisley, Cameron

# the fab two-in-one dining room

It's always impressive to see starter apartments where so much attention (and precious square footage) is focused on being able to entertain. This area is 16 x 13 feet, which is plenty large for a dining room on its own but pretty compact when a living room shares the same footprint.

The sofa sits opposite the table, allowing for as much open area as possible between the two largest pieces of furniture in the room. Selecting the right dining table was key here. It has unusually small proportions. With the leaves down, it's the size of a card table and fits snugly in front of the large window. When extended, however, the long table seats as many as eight people comfortably. The rest of the furnishings are mobile: dining chairs turn to face the coffee table when guests arrive, and the bar can be scooted around (or out of) the room.

Over-the-table lighting was skipped in favor of a striking metallic (faux) antler chandelier. Hanging one statement light fixture in the center of the room, instead of using multiple smaller lights in the dining and living areas, helps unify the multipurpose space even more.

BROOKLYN
Taylor Swaim
Brand Creative

**DREAM BIGGER.** This rich palette is a nod to the homeowner's style inspiration, Jenna Lyons, J.Crew's Executive Creative Director. Lyons's former Brooklyn brownstone was done in shades of gray, white, and black, which are elegantly imitated here.

**14**

kitchens

**BACKSPLASH BARGAINS.** (LEFT) This thrifty couple trekked all the way to Sausalito, California, to shop the "overstock" selection at Heath Ceramics, their dream tile source. If your design is flexible, most tile stores have a discount section where great deals can be found.

**KNOCK. KNOCK.** (OPPOSITE) This extra-long table is actually an old door the homeowners had kicking around their art studio. They sanded it down, added legs, and left the top unfinished so that its rustic charm continues to get better with age.

# the retro bright kitchen

The '70s are alive and kicking in this sunny Elysian Park kitchen. Every detail, from the custom cabinetry (handcrafted by the homeowner) to the cork flooring to the retro color palette, is a nod to streamlined, midcentury design.

What you don't see in this photo are the gorgeous gardens just beyond a set of massive sliding glass doors (skip to chapter 19 for a peek). The pale blue, deep green, and pops of orange bring the explosion of natural color happening outside in, making a space of mostly neutrals seem highly saturated.

When embracing a design period so fully, it's important to realize that not everything should be vintage. This hardworking kitchen does a nice job of balancing old and new. The teak veneer cabinets, Heath Ceramics tile backsplash, and cork floor are all new. The Wedgewood stove is vintage on the outside but has been upgraded with modern technology inside, while the dining chairs and most of the ceramics collection (the black vessel above the cabinets is the homeowner's own work) are vintage through and through. A good rule of thumb to follow: frequently used pieces should be new, while decorative or less-used items provide an opportunity to sprinkle in vintage treasures.

LOS ANGELES
**Judy Kameon + Erik Otsea**
Landscape Designer +
Outdoor Furniture Designer
son, Ian

**KITCHEN COMMANDO.** Realizing that her happiest hours were spent in the kitchen, Judy had a small workstation built in to the far corner of the room. The secretary-style desk closes up when guests arrive.

# the beach cottage kitchen

The genius of this superlight, minimalist kitchen is in how quickly and affordably it was assembled. When the homeowners purchased this small cottage on stilts (which sits directly on the bay in Long Island), they needed to get it fixed up as fast as possible for as little as possible.

Sticking with basics, like an all-white palette and IKEA cabinetry, meant that everything could be installed in just two weeks. (That's lightning-speed by typical home-renovation standards.) Custom floating shelves keep the walls open and the kitchen nice and airy. Exposed storage like this only works if you trust yourself to organize your dishes neatly. Mismatched sets or overstuffed shelves are an instant eyesore.

Solid wood countertops add warmth to the all-white space—and will age well if oiled regularly. Bright artwork and little graphic touches (an owl cookie jar, patterned serving trays) provide the fun spark that really brings this room to life.

If you want to keep your space light and open, and storage is not a big issue, this is a great little kitchen to get inspired by.

EAST HAMPTON, NY
**Christiane Lemieux + Joshua Young**
Founder, DwellStudio + Real Estate Developer
daughter, Isabelle + son, William

**MAKE A SPLASH.** For a crisp, modern look, nothing beats a white subway tile backsplash. This one was installed in straight, slightly offset lines that accentuate the gorgeous length of the kitchen.

# the never-at-rest kitchen

This is what a chef's kitchen really looks like: a little bit messy (because it's never not in use) but a total workhorse that's so cozy, you'd happily spend every waking hour in it.

Though modest in size, this kitchen offers plenty of counter space for food prep, two full-sized refrigerators, and a large farmhouse sink. But what's even more key to its overall function is the layout: the commercial range and sink are both located in the center of the room, so you can pivot in any direction while cooking and reach the countertop, the faucet, or a pot on the stove.

Off both ends of the room are two additional spaces, one for sitting and one for storage—and every square inch is used. Part of the charm of this kitchen is its many flights of whimsy, which spill into these extra areas: deep blue cabinets, palm-frond wallpaper, vintage signage, and collected figurines. There is a smart mix of what is necessary for cooking and what is necessary for inspiring creativity—a good example of balancing playfulness with function in any space.

LOS ANGELES
Lulu Powers + Stephen Danelian
The Entertainologist + Founder, MeeLocal

**COOKING UP A STORM.** With a six-burner commercial stove and baker-grade oven, this comfortable kitchen can cook for a lot more than one family. Having that type of fire power costs more but is money well spent for the ambitious home chef.

**KICK YOUR FEET UP.** (LEFT) Offering a view into the busy kitchen, this lovely small sitting room—with its cozy green armchairs, tropical print ottoman, and palm frond wallpaper—is a welcome retreat while waiting for the oven timer to ding.

**BEST VIEW IN THE HOUSE.** (ABOVE) Big porcelain farm sinks are having a moment—and it's easy to see why. They hold a ton of dishes, stay clean with minimal elbow grease, and are especially dreamy when placed under a sunny window.

# the neapolitan kitchen

Who would ever imagine that such a hardworking room could be inspired by the colors of Neapolitan ice cream? But day-in-and-day-out meals for a family of six are whipped up in this lighthearted kitchen with chocolate countertops (the starting point for the design), strawberry pink cabinets, and vanilla walls.

The biggest takeaway here is that if you're brave enough to try an off-the-beaten-path style, really embrace it. Don't just paint the cabinets;

**TWO (OR THREE) OF A KIND.**
(LEFT) When choosing accent colors, be sure to include at least two examples of it—like the blue and yellow here—so it feels intentional.

BARRINGTON, IL
**Michelle + Dave Kohanzo**
CEO, Land of Nod + Banker
daughter, Emily + sons Connor, Henry, Everett

**THE SWEETEST DETAILS.** (CENTER) Antique wallpaper was added as a backdrop to the hutch; a simple detail that really delivers.

**THE POWER OF PAINT.** (RIGHT) To gain a bit of vintage-y goodness, a thrift store hutch was painted to match the standard cabinetry.

paint the rest of the furniture, too. Don't just baby step into the ice-cream-parlor vibe; dive into it with loads of retro details: paper garlands, gingham patterns, '50s-style-diner dishes, and wall art that declares a love of cake. Half measures will only result in a watered-down version. This type of decorative daring takes guts. But, mainly, it's an important reminder that you shouldn't be too serious, especially with decor; being memorable is way more fun.

**KITCHEN FOLIAGE.** Homes glow when they include fresh flowers and plants. The tulips and potted succulents sprinkled around this kitchen lift spirits during post-meal dishwashing.

## the western soda-fountain kitchen

The only thing missing from this modern rustic kitchen is a set of swinging saloon doors. Equal parts new finishings and reclaimed flea market finds (one of the homeowners restores vintage furniture for a living), this open, high-traffic, eat-in kitchen brings a little bit of the Old West to Venice Beach.

A white-on-white palette and multiple windows serve as a foundation for the bright, clean look. Details like vintage swivel stools, industrial lighting, and dark, hand-poured concrete countertops add a rough-and-tumble sophistication, while the pin-striping in the beadboard on the lower half of the room snaps everything into focus.

The key to this space is the nicely balanced, U-shaped flow. This kitchen serves a large family with older children, so the stream of hungry people is constant. A four-seater counter faces a large commercial range, centering the room. Expansive countertops and two sinks—one in front of the window, the other in the island— mean that multiple people can prepare food at once. And extra outlets built directly into the island serve as a power station for all the electronics that get abandoned there.

VENICE BEACH
Susan + Kevin Lennon
Owner, SHOP by h. bleu + Founder, Lennon Design
daughter, Griffin

# the collector's bazaar kitchen

There are many kinds of cooks—and many ways to set up a kitchen. More "workshop" than "lab," this one belongs to an artist. All the culinary tools are left out within arm's reach for the moment inspiration strikes: pots hang from the ceiling, cutting boards run up the wall, and open, industrial shelves house all manner of cookware and serving pieces.

In truth, there's little rhyme or reason to the placement of things; it's simply a reflection of the homeowners and how they use this space. The dark-wood countertops and shelving were a DIY project—and the industrial island was tacked on for added surface space. But perhaps the greatest thing about this room (aside from its deep blue hue) is how lived-in and loved it feels.

It's as "busy" as a commercial kitchen, but nothing is either too sterile-looking or precious. A small sitting area between the wood-burning stove and windows provides a front-row seat to all the action. Art and carefully curated objects, like the European glass flycatchers that dangle above the stove, make the space feel old-fashioned and homey.

For all the advice out there on organizing a kitchen, sometimes—clearly—it pays to go your own way.

**THE PERFECT SHADE.** (LEFT)
When you fall in love with a paint color, it's a hard thing to let go of. This vibrant blue (Benjamin Moore "Blue Belle") is a holdover from Michele's previous kitchen—and according to her, will be in all of her kitchens to come.

**NOWHERE TO HIDE.** (ABOVE)
With every last dish in plain sight, this room shows off its treasures (like this collection of bowls from Pearl River) while making it easier to sort through the eclectic feast.

**THE LOCKER ROOM.** (OPPOSITE)
With nothing but open storage, this kitchen lacked a place to stash the actual food, so this rusty old locker was smartly turned into a makeshift pantry.

NEW YORK CITY
**Michele Varian + Brad Roberts**
Shop Owner, Michele Varian + Musician

**HANG IT HIGHER.** Ceilings can provide very effective storage solutions. Beyond the hanging glass flycatchers, the commercial pot rack forms a central hub, keeping every pan within arm's reach.

# the smart-storage kitchen

This chef-grade kitchen sits in what used to be an electrical switching station. (Semitrucks drove through here.) So it feels somewhat appropriate that in its modern iteration, the stainless-steel kitchen is still very much an industrial space.

Any room that relies on exposed beams and cement floors for charm risks coming off as cold. But the details that could be considered "chilly" (glazed-brick walls and rows of metal cabinets) are balanced by the long wall of warm, wood-toned cabinetry and personality-packed lighting choices: an illuminated *S* (from a Singer sewing machine sign) and a wall-mounted fixture that swivels to provide light when and where it's needed.

Technically, these cabinets are clothing wardrobes. But the inventive homeowner uses them for kitchen storage. Matching sets of glasses are meticulously lined up next to perfectly stacked plates and serving dishes. One entire cupboard is dedicated to bar accessories, another to coffee and tea supplies, and a third to cookware. Just enough space is left between collections to avoid overcrowding. This impressive level of detail adds a very human touch to the laboratory-like setting.

CHICAGO
Lisa + Joel Santos
Gourmet Grocer/Chef + Computer Developer

**STORAGE AS ART.** This bank of wardrobes provides an amazing amount of storage, but that's only half the story. Lisa created an art-installation-like backdrop to her dining area by keeping like-size items together and not over-packing the shelves.

**HIGH + LOW DONE RIGHT.** (OPPOSITE)
Stainless steel cabinetry, arranged in an island
configuration, looks high-end but isn't, leaving
room in the budget for a standout light fixture.
Prouvé's Potence swivel lamp is a classic.

**YOUR HOME, YOUR HOBBIES.** (ABOVE)
Lisa and Joel love to cook, so having easy
access to their most essential tools makes
this kitchen "just right" for them. Factoring
your passions into your design plans will
always result in a place where you want to
spend time.

**WORKING WINDOWS.** The couple's large utensils hang from hooks on a metal rod in the window; it's a small investment that's both attractive and handy.

# the little kitchen that could

This kitchen packs an amazing amount of function into a perfectly designed, not-an-inch-wasted, 120 square feet. The modern country galley is a brilliant illustration of the perennial wisdom about small homes: make the most of your vertical space.

With a slope from 6 feet at the windows to 10 feet on the opposite side, the ceiling allows for a full floor-to-ceiling wall of open storage—accessible via a rolling ladder. Extra-deep shelves are packed with a tremendous collection of dishes, glassware, cooking tools, and entertaining essentials.

Having everything out within arm's (or, in this case, ladder's) reach is great, but keeping all those little items clean is another story. The simple solution? Use them! It ensures they cycle through the dishwasher regularly—and is an excellent excuse for entertaining.

Unconventional work surfaces are another great small-space solution. Rather than out-of-the-box cabinets, the homeowners found affordable custom options. One is a wooden media console topped with Carrara marble, and the other, a stainless-steel table, was sourced from a restaurant-supply fabricator in a height that accommodates a wine fridge and dishwasher underneath.

AUSTIN
Tim Cuppett + Marco Rini
Architect + Garden Designer

**JUST ROLL WITH IT.** (ABOVE) Ladders and china may seem like a tricky combo, but these homeowners (wisely) store fragile items on lower shelves and, as an extra precaution, chose a ladder with deep rungs that can hold dishes while they climb.

**NO CABINETS. NO PROBLEM.** (CENTER) Wall-hung cookware, coffee cup hooks, and an ingenious plate rack make alternative storage solutions seem like a design plus rather than a necessary evil.

**WARM MEMORIES.** (ABOVE) Marco studied in England, living in a chilly bedsit with a trusty Aga cooker. When it came time to choose a range for the cottage, going with this classic brand was a no-brainer.

# the carefully curated kitchen

Think about everything that happens in your kitchen (preparing food, having meals, entertaining). Now think about doing that in less than 100 square feet.

It takes discipline to keep a kitchen this pared down and still be inspired to cook in it. Editing yourself to the most basic kitchen essentials can be incredibly freeing, though. Fewer things mean your options are automatically limited. You know which recipes you have the tools to make, how many people fit comfortably at your table, and so forth.

But editing is only part of what makes this chic little kitchen so hardworking. There's stealth utility everywhere you look. Shelves were added to all the walls. Dry foods are shifted into clear glass containers upon purchase (which helps minimize visual clutter). And the dishes are kept in neat rows or stacked.

To create fluidity among all these mismatched elements, everything was covered in flat white paint—giving it a "built-in" look. A small round dining table allows for maximum movement through the space, while one dark half wall and a framed photograph of Iceland (taken by the homeowner) turn the eat-in nook into the coziest spot in the house.

NEW YORK CITY
Emily Johnston
Photographer

**THE DARK SIDE.** This kitchen's moody character is all thanks to its deep gray accents (Benjamin Moore's "Deep River"), which jump from the bathroom door to the wall (at right).

**DISHING IT OUT.** (OPPOSITE) The curving shapes and off-white tones of Emily's dishes allow everything to sit together harmoniously, even though the design sources are all over the place: Virginia Sin, Heath Ceramics, Simon Pearce, even IKEA.

**A PLACE FOR EVERYTHING.** (ABOVE) IKEA shelving and simple, open boxes mounted on the walls provide all the storage this kitchen needs at a minimal expense. Hanging cubbies for flatware eliminate the need for a drawer.

**WHO NEEDS STARBUCKS?** (LEFT)
This adorable, color-coded coffee
station is a caffeine lover's dream.
Storing "like" items (coffee mugs,
coffeemaker, teapot, and so forth)
in one spot increases a room's
functionality instantly.

**COUNTER CULTURE.** (OPPOSITE)
Try as she might to keep her
countertops clutter-free, Taylor
found that stuff just seemed to
accumulate there. Rather than
fight it, she embraced it and
purchased pretty bowls and a
utensil jar to capture everything
neatly.

# the diy kitchen

Just because you live in a rental doesn't mean you can't have a bright,
happy, personalized kitchen you want to spend time in.

This galley kitchen in Brooklyn was dirty and run-down when the
renter first moved in. A lot of energy was put into turning it around on a
dime. The landlord agreed to replace the worn linoleum floor—and gave
permission for the cabinets to be painted. Using a cabinet-refinishing kit
by Rust-Oleum, the cheap blond cabinets (which you find in most affordable rentals) were updated into the stylish gray fronts you see here.

The old backsplash was also in bad shape. Rather than paint over the
broken tiles (which never works well) or replace them (too expensive),
plastic ceiling tiles from Home Depot—which are meant to look like tin—
were cut and stuck to the surface with super-adhesive double-sided tape.
The subtle shine and hit of texture adds a low-key vintage feel.

When faced with a space that's been neglected for years (or even
decades), clean it up, fix what needs fixing, and do whatever refinishing
you can. No matter what style you "inherit," you'll find that good energy
will return to your home once the clutter and grime are gone and everything is in working order.

BROOKLYN
Taylor Swaim
Brand Creative

**DON'T WORRY ABOUT WHAT THE RULES SAY.**
By most accounts, this little dining area would
be located in the center of a room with space for
the chairs to scoot into and away from the table.
But this configuration, as it turns out, is far more
laidback and inviting.

# 8 THINGS NOT to worry about

**1 TRENDS.** If you love design, trend-spotting can be inspiring and, frankly, good fun (especially when you become enough of an expert to see them coming). But what a trend should never be is a deal breaker. True style is about confidence, so following your heart, whether something is "on trend" or not, is always going to yield the most powerful results.

**2 A ROOM'S INTENDED PURPOSE.** Want to use that small, dark guest bedroom as the closet of your dreams? Maybe switch the living room and the dining room? Or how about turning the dining nook into a home office? Go for it. Use the space in your home so it makes the most sense for how you live day to day.

**3 WHAT YOUR FRIENDS THINK.** Good friends give advice; it's part of the deal and always worth considering. But when it comes to choosing your home, or the things that go into it, only you know what will make you happy. If a pale, monochromatic living room is your ideal, don't let naysayers chattering about difficult upkeep change your mind. Your true friends will come around.

**4 STOCKING UP.** Take these wise words to heart: store it at the store. Don't turn your home into a stockroom. Sure, having whatever you need on hand when you need it gives you a good feeling. But using precious space for a year's supply of toilet paper is not the way to do it. A much better strategy: spend an extra few minutes a week maintaining a shopping list.

**5 BEING THE PERFECT HOST.** Think back to the most fun you've had as a guest in someone's home. Was it because the host anticipated your every wish, serving gourmet food in a pristine room? Of course not. Your guests will only feel sincerely welcome when you stop worrying and start enjoying yourself.

**6 WHAT THE RULES SAY.** The fashion world insists you shouldn't wear white after Labor Day. Similarly, there are a handful of decorating "rules," which, in all honesty, are often worth following: hanging art 57 to 60 inches on center, for instance (for more on this see chapter 9). But if you have an urge to break the rules, be a rebel. How will you know if hanging your art higher isn't the brilliant exception to the rule until you try it?

**7 REGRETTING LETTING GO.** Our minds can be tricky about getting rid of stuff; we convince ourselves we may need an item *someday*, when the truth is, we don't use it . . . ever. Clearing clutter is always a good thing. Give yourself permission to let things go by focusing on the next owner who will use and enjoy the item.

**8 STARTING OVER.** You were positive you were going to love that "_____." (Fill in the blank: bold wall color, ornate vintage mirror, ruffled bedspread.) Now, after living with it, you realize that it's still not working. There's no embarrassment in admitting a design misstep. Repainting or returning/selling an item and going back to square one is better than putting up with something you don't love. Live and learn!

work
spaces

# the closet-office

Necessity breeds creativity—especially when you're trying to fit a substantial work space into a tiny, 430-square-foot apartment. This resourceful homeowner's solution was to turn an awkwardly shaped hallway and closet into an office with storage galore.

This space works because of the built-in desk surface lining the wall. Coated in a light gray, it provides a large work platform while taking up very little of the actual room. In small areas like this, built-in elements are always the best option.

Behind the desk, one closet was turned into floor-to-ceiling storage by removing the door and adding elfa shelving. (When guests come over, the whole thing is hidden behind a curtain.) The solutions continue under the desk, which houses two file cabinets that can easily be wheeled out when more surface area is needed. A set of large white magnet boards on the wall showcase the homeowner's constantly changing sources of inspiration.

If you're having a function-versus-space struggle, start by listing your "wants" in order of necessity. If something is truly a priority, you'll find room for it.

**LABEL MASTER.** (ABOVE) As a photographer, Emily deals with large amounts of data stored across multiple hard drives. The key to her filing system? Labels! She names every hard drive and every file.

**WIDTH OVER DEPTH.** (OPPOSITE) Next time you're in the market for a desk, keep this in mind: having a wide surface tends to be more helpful than a deep one because it keeps everything in plain sight.

NEW YORK CITY
Emily Johnston
Photographer

# a color-coded office

Even the smallest slice of room can be transformed into a successful work space as long as it ticks the boxes you need to stay motivated: a bit of privacy for focus, plenty of light to keep spirits up, and enough storage space that your projects stay organized and your desktop remains neat and clean.

Technically, this sunny office is nothing more than a small platform connecting the home's main stairwell to its rooftop deck. But thanks to some smart space planning, it functions as a full-time work space. A shallow, inexpensive desk provides just enough room for the computer station. Pieced together from two gray metal cabinets and a cut-to-size white countertop, this DIY desk is purposely placed in front of the windows for a fantastic view of the neighboring treetops.

The rest of the long, narrow space is used solely for storage. Not an inch is wasted, with a floor-to-ceiling installation of simple, wall-mounted shelving. Books are used for both information and inspiration. Color-coded, clearly labeled storage boxes—of various shapes and sizes—house everything from magazines to business contracts. And a few family treasures keep the highly functional office from veering too far into "all work" territory.

CHICAGO
**Brenda + David Bergen**
Graphic Designer + Digital Media Consultant
son, Daniel

**TINY TREASURES.** Even in a compact space organized for maximum efficiency, you should find some room for a plant. This one enjoys the view from above on a wall-mounted ledge.

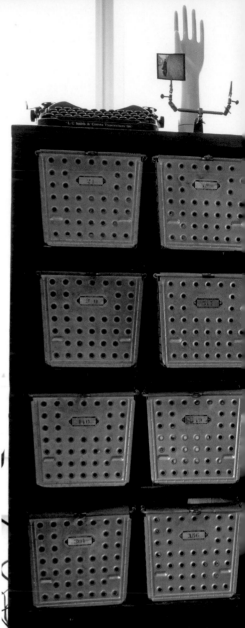

# the den of creativity

A creative person's office is easy to spot. It bucks the traditional elements and, instead, is built to spark thought and artistic energy.

This space is a wonderful example of just that: all the furniture is vintage, but it comes from multiple eras. A mid-century modern Eames chair sits next to a nineteenth-century French side chair paired with a unit of metal storage cabinets found at an abandoned school in New Orleans (currently being used as a makeshift filing system for delicate work). The mix of designs makes for an intriguing juxtaposition that's also a lot less formal than the typical set of matching office furniture.

**WRINKLE FREE.** (LEFT) Interesting collections come in all shapes and sizes. This couple happens to have a thing for tiny antique irons, which line the window frame behind the desk.

BROOKLYN
Moon Rhee + Heyja Do
Shop Owners, Dear: Rivington+

**SEND OUT THE BAT SIGNAL.**
(CENTER) On top of this storage
cabinet sits a hard-to-find Batman
figurine. Amidst all the "serious"
supplies, a nod to Gotham's finest
is a nice change of pace.

**DIY ART.** (RIGHT) This painting,
done by Moon in the style of
Willem de Kooning, is one of a
few in the home that successfully
mimic iconic pieces.

The drawback to a lot of creative spaces is that they can very quickly
become messy and overcrowded. But the fashion designers who live
here do a lovely job of curating this joint office. The clusters of interesting objects have been thought through and considered. And while
there is a lot going on, there is a lot of carefully preserved empty space,
too. Collections are only as powerful as your ability to focus on them.
Too many objects without breathing room will be more distracting than
inspiring.

**TRIPLE STACK.** (LEFT) Clara von Zweigbergk's Kaleido trays (spread across the desk and file cabinet here) are a color explosion of function and fun. They serve as a catchall for tiny pieces when assembling a project, or a tabletop art installation on every other day.

**PIN IT.** (OPPOSITE) Anne's black-and-white inspiration board, a throwback to the days before Pinterest, is lovingly collected from magazine clippings, fashion show invites, and photo booth pictures.

# the sun porch–turned-office

The moment these newbie house hunters laid eyes on this light-filled room, they knew it was the place for them. Where most people saw a sun porch, this couple saw the home office of their dreams.

With two floor-to-ceiling glass doors, each opening onto its own balcony, and an entire wall of windows, this office feels equal parts indoors and out—a perk that they take full advantage of. More often than not, the doors and windows are left open to let in the California breeze.

Almost all the furniture is streamlined, industrial, and most important, white. It blends right into the walls, taking up little visual space in the already narrow room. The single exception is an overstuffed armchair decked out in a wild Josef Frank fabric (one half of a matching set that's split between this space and the living room). Just behind the chair is what could be called an "extra office on wheels": a long table and filing cabinet that are rolled in to accommodate more work stations during busy times of year.

The real "wow" factor of this room, though, comes from its restraint. In a sea of white-on-white, a few fun pops of highlighter-pink and cerulean blue, as well as some graphic black-and-white art, bring the whole space to life.

LOS ANGELES
Anne Ziegler + Scott Mason
Trend Forecaster + Entertainment Executive

**STICKS & STONES.** (LEFT)
Keeping with the woodsy theme, these homeowners had some fun with their interpretation of desk supplies: pencils are made of twigs, letter openers are painted like feathers, and found rocks double as paperweights.

**IN THE CLEAR.** (OPPOSITE)
Mounting a French swivel light on the wall, instead of having a lamp on the desk, clears precious surface space for laptops and keyboards.

# an office with a view

Essentially, this tiny work space is nothing more than a narrow desk, a chair, and a wall-mounted lamp. It's squeezed tightly into the corner of an open but small living space (roughly 400 square feet) that also contains the kitchen, living room, and dining room. So how did the homeowner keep sitting in this nook from feeling like an adult time-out? The nice, light-filled window.

Sometimes no amount of creative floor planning and multifunctional furniture can create the additional space you're after—especially in a high-traffic room like this. But if you have a window, placing a desk directly in front of it is the best way to sneak in some office space. The expansive view outside makes up for the lack of room inside.

The strategic use of color is an equally smart, visually space-saving solution here. Matching the largest pieces of furniture (the desk and chair) with the shade of the natural Douglas fir walls helps the office "blend" into the corner, minimizing clutter in the room. A few well-placed pieces of art make this an inspiring spot to work.

ELIZAVILLE, NY
Christopher Coleman +
Angel Sanchez
Interior Designer + Fashion Designer

# the artist's work table

This is not a neat and tidy office. All manner of art supplies are scattered across the desk. Even more scraps of fabric, bits of yarn, and rolls of decorative paper line a nearby set of extra-tall industrial shelves. And tiny, inspirational odds and ends fill stacks of decorative boxes on the floor. But if you ask the artist and designer who works here what goes where, she can pinpoint every last paintbrush and square inch of ribbon.

There's a method to the madness of this contained chaos—one that might only make sense to its creator, but, in reality, that's the only person who matters. At the center of it all is a large, smoothly worn table with enough space for multiple projects to be laid out at once. The pillow-filled window seat serves as a sort of home base, but the spacious nook is built for movement. There's plenty of open area to stand up and scoot around the table, working on one project, then focusing on the next.

A room like this is a glimpse at an artist in motion. The creative process dictates the placement of every detail—and that is a beautiful thing.

**NEW YORK CITY**
Michele Varian + Brad Roberts
Shop Owner, Michele Varian + Musician

**PILLOW TALK.** The pillows that line this cozy corner nook are all the homeowner's own creations. The large felted bird in the corner has become a signature design for her store.

**16**

bedrooms

# a novel bedroom

Inspired by Ernest Hemingway's historic home in Key West, this bedroom is a magnetic mix of rustic details and pop-y polka dots. Quirky references to animals of the hunt are sprinkled throughout: a trio of bird images (the thrifty homeowner tore them right out of a book) hang over the bed, ceramic owls perch on the dresser, and a papier-mâché stag overlooks the bedside desk.

But the real star of this room is the polka-dot-sheet-covered bed. It's always a good idea to center your bed against the largest uninterrupted wall. This immediately helps with balance and flow in a space. Here, with the splashy spots commanding your attention, the bed becomes the visual centerpiece not only of this room, but of the adjoining living/dining room, as well.

The play of dots against plaid and ruched cotton against heavy wool creates a beautiful, dramatic moment. So the rest of the room is kept light and airy: the walls, curtains, and vintage furniture are all a pale shade. The only true color comes from a set of rich red Persian rugs that flank the bed, a last nod to the lodgelike Hemingway home.

BROOKLYN
Taylor Swaim
Brand Creative

**ALL THE TRIMMINGS. (OPPOSITE)** These old walls are rough, but they look crisp thanks to all the well-kept original molding, a detail that adds dimension and a sense of grandeur to any room.

**JEWELRY JUMBLE. (ABOVE)** This jewelry tree is buried in personality. Stands like this are an excellent way to stop watches, small accessories, and scarves from becoming a tangled mountain on your dresser.

# the surf shack bedroom

This backyard pavilion in Venice Beach was puzzle-pieced together on the cheap. It is constructed almost entirely from architectural salvage; hence, the front wall of beautifully mismatched windows. The handy homeowners quickly assembled the makeshift home when their main residence was being renovated—and it has since become a landing spot for family, friends, and roaming surfers.

Taking up one side of this open studio space, the bedroom faces a set of antique doors that flood the room with light. Flowering vines have pushed through the rear cinder-block walls and are growing up and out. While the architectural details and ceiling are all painted a clean, bright white, the rear beams are dark blue, and the front wall is made from repurposed wood planks (stripped from old factory dollies).

The plywood floors were also painted. Oversize black and white squares were placed at an angle (like diamonds) instead of lined up (like rectangles) with the room—a great trick for creating visual movement while avoiding the static feeling of a common checkerboard alignment.

Every mostly white room needs contrasts like these; they make the difference between a sterile space and one that's full of warmth and life.

VENICE BEACH
Susan + Kevin Lennon
Owner, SHOP by h. bleu + Founder, Lennon Design
daughter, Griffin

**CURTAIN CALL.** Sheer white curtains are casually suspended from a thin rod, almost as if they were hanging in the sun to dry. This is a super-affordable treatment that allows for privacy while keeping the mood soft and romantic.

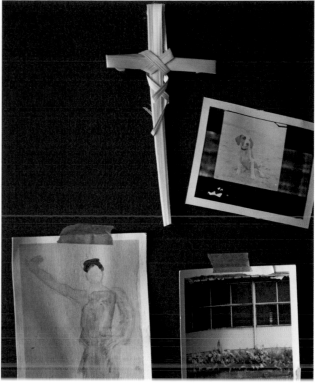

# the dark & cozy hideout

What do you do when you have a long, thin railroad apartment and no clear spot for a bedroom? You redefine your definition of "bedroom." This homeowner tucked her bed into a small alcove off the main hallway where it is cozy, quiet, and dark. Technically not a room at all, this tiny space is just deep enough for a full-size mattress—and nothing more.

To define the alcove, so it didn't feel like an awkward cell, three changes were made. The interior walls and ceiling were painted a deep gray-blue, cloaking the space in comforting darkness and separating it from the other rooms. A platform-bed frame was built to fill the entire nook and provide storage underneath. And the third masterstroke was hanging tall curtains to give it a little more privacy—and a lot more light control for sleeping.

An oversize surprise always helps a small space. Here, it's the nice big brass pendant light over the bed, as well as the optional hammock, which works as an additional bed for guests or the occasional afternoon nap.

**HAMMOCK-VILLE.** (LEFT) Hung on two large hooks and securely bolted to the walls, this hammock (a souvenir from France) is a favorite retreat from work. Because you can't type in a hammock . . . you just can't.

**SIMPLE SNAPS.** (RIGHT) In opposition to all her nicely framed art, a postcard, two Polaroids, and a handmade grass cross are taped to the wall in a hurried but personal gesture.

**A MOROCCAN ALCOVE.** (OPPOSITE) Instead of two curtains, Emily hung three—which makes all the difference. Two panels can come off as youthful, while three feels sophisticated.

NEW YORK CITY
Emily Johnston
Photographer

**VIEW FROM THE TOP.** The exaggerated height of the metal bedframe is mirrored in Artemide's modern "Tolomeo" desk lamp. It's this common ground that makes mixing pieces from different eras successful.

# the garden view bedroom

It may sound counterintuitive to design a space based on a view, but this ethereal, second-floor bedroom was dictated by that very principle.

The metal, almost museum-like bed sits against the middle of a wall with sweeping views of the gardens it overlooks. Even its unusual height is meant to maximize the line of vision through the windows. And placing the large worktable directly in front of the bed means that the homeowner can enjoy the same sight lines while working.

The rest of the room, which doubles as a home office, is purposely left minimal. Nearly bare floors, flat white paint, and shade-less windows define the look of the master suite. A single painting (of the homeowner as a teen) and a vintage rug add just a hint of personalization. The result: a spare, modern sensibility crossed with a spare, old-fashioned style.

Not every room can be led by a view, but what lies outside your windows should be taken into account. Spend some time looking at the sights from various angles around your space. You could catch a glimpse of a favorite tree or building and end up nudging a chair over a few inches to enjoy it.

EAST COAST
Deborah Nevins
Landscape Designer

# the old hollywood bedroom

Saturated colors, intricate patterns, and dark wood are all throwbacks to the old Hollywood era. There is something comforting in the richness of these details, and something playful in the way they come together here.

This bedroom is extremely formal on the surface, with a neatly centered bed, thinly piped starched sheets, picture lights perched atop framed artwork, and acres of pillows. A mahogany-colored faux-fur throw echoes the brown wood trim, while old paintings add a museum-like quality to the space.

But the dominant use of sunny yellow gives the whole room more of a laid-back, beach house vibe. Gauzy, whisper-thin curtains increase the airiness. Even the toile wallpaper is a contemporary version of the classic print updated with muted shades of gray-blue set against a yolk-y background.

This lighthearted approach to design is crucial to keeping the fun versus formal balance in check. The last thing you want in a bedroom meant for relaxing is a space that takes itself too seriously.

LOS ANGELES
Lulu Powers + Stephen Danelian
The Entertainologist + Founder, MeeLocal

**KEEP THEM GUESSING.** A furry brown blanket is just the thing to throw off all these bright whites and sunny yellows. This rustic touch keeps the room from tilting too far in one design direction.

# the french boudoir

This sun-drenched master bedroom is entirely about the wallpaper. Rolls of the hand-painted de Gournay design took six months to arrive, and, the homeowner likes to joke, "cost about a year's salary." It was a big-ticket item that she saved for and dreamed about for years. So every other design element in the room plays off its whimsical style.

The wall-to-wall carpeting (always a good choice for bedrooms) has a sweet, subtle, floral texture that's soft underfoot and practically renders the room silent. A metal canopy bed from Restoration Hardware, upholstered with a graphic pink fabric, picks up the pattern in the rug and softens the room even more. Luxuriously full silk curtains hang floor-to-ceiling, adding the illusion of height to the cropped walls.

Storage for this room is neatly hidden away. The only dresser doubles as a side table for the bed, while the full wall of closets is disguised behind wallpaper-covered doors. The rest of the space is pared down and minimal, so your full attention always remains on the dreamy scene playing across the walls.

LOS ANGELES
Ruthie Sommers + Luke McDonough
Interior Designer + CEO, AirMedia
daughters Eloise, Bailey, Posey

EVERY INCH COUNTS. Notice how the width of this bed matches the width of the windows behind it perfectly. This was not an accident. The precise fit reduces visual clutter in the open space.

**CAPTURED MOMENTS. (LEFT)** Photographs of children are priceless, but when framed well they transition from family keepsakes to true art.

**DOUBLE DOWN. (OPPOSITE)** This lovely quilt features a graphic print on one side and thin stripes on the other, meaning you can switch up the whole mood of the room simply by flipping over the blanket.

# the blissed-out master suite

If you have the space, a great headboard quickly establishes a bold style. Minimal changes have been made to this room: the walls were painted pale lavender, and a big graphic silk and wool rug was plopped down. The room is radiant, simply because of the shimmering tufted velvet bed that sits right in the middle of it all.

This glowing bedroom is located on the seventeenth floor of a prewar apartment building overlooking Lake Michigan. With older buildings like this, the built-in features—generous proportions, dark wood floors, and thick molding—are the main attractions. In particular, the windows, with their decorative guardrails, feel like artwork and bathe the room in light that changes throughout the day. Filling the space with furniture that detracts attention from these elements would be a mistake.

Less is more here; the massive, curving headboard gets to be the main style statement in a room already rife with built-in personality.

CHICAGO
Eric Oliver + Thea Goodman
Professor + Author
daughter, Esme + son, Ethan

**H-ART.** This photo collage was made from a few favorite family pics the homeowner had professionally printed.

# the world-of-whimsy bedroom

Can a master suite also be the heart of a family home? According to this playground of a bedroom, the answer is a resounding . . . absolutely! Rather than a grown-ups-only sanctuary, it works as a movie-night hangout and lazy-Sunday lounging zone for the family of six.

Light, bright, and upbeat, the room's decor reflects an eye for sophisticated detail and a quirky sense of humor. Playful touches, such as a vintage German Marilyn Monroe movie poster and a heart-shaped collage made from a year's worth of travel photos, keep things lighthearted.

All the extra seating is the key to why this sunny room doesn't fall into disarray after so much use. Aside from a giant king bed, there's a pink settee and a chair loaded up with blankets for making cozy piles on the floor. The overall impression is comfortable, layered, and lush, with a refined but soft palette and a rich array of textures, from the velvet settee to the textured rug to the furry gray pillows on the bed.

This is a space that truly defines what it is to have a "happy home."

**INSTANT GRATIFICATION.** (LEFT) A fast, easy, inexpensive way to get a poster on the wall without making holes in the paper: extra-large bulldog clips hung from tiny nails!

**SITTING PRETTY.** (CENTER) This bedside table is larger than most but has to be extremely hardworking. It's a landing spot for jewelry, toys, magazines, and the family's cat.

**WHAT TO WEAR?** (RIGHT) Michelle's curtain rod doubles as a landing spot for possible outfit contenders. As a welcome side effect, her fashion becomes a fun part of the room's decor.

BARRINGTON, IL
**Michelle + Dave Kohanzo**
CEO, Land of Nod + Banker
daughter, Emily +
sons Connor, Henry, Everett

# the minimalist master suite

Some people like to sleep in big bedrooms; others prefer the intimate retreat of tight quarters. This all-white space offers a great example of the latter. Located in the smallest room of a spacious duplex in downtown Brooklyn, the footprint of this bedroom might be tiny, but the level of coziness is through the roof.

To counteract the tightness of the space, the king bed sits right on the floor, lowering the "waistline" of the room. This drastically opens the top half of the space, making the walls seem taller and the ceiling farther away.

An all-white palette also helps expand the room. The white used on the walls here, a very bright "photographer's white," has a cool, modern feel. Soft, textural layers add contrast: a piece of antique lace drapes the bed, and an even older scrap of framed lace rests on the windowsill.

With all that white, some darker elements are needed for definition. An antique side table from Kenya, a rubber tree, and a vintage desk lamp become small, impactful moments. But the most eye-catching element of all is the unframed black line painting (created by the homeowner with a little bit of house paint)—a lovely, personal focal point in the sparse bedroom.

BROOKLYN
Moon Rhee + Heyja Do
Shop Owners, Dear: Rivington+

**PILLOW TOWER.** In most homes you expect to find colorful throw pillows sitting side by side across the top of the bed. But here, in a refreshing twist, the all-white pillows are stacked, biggest to smallest.

# the stargazer's lounge

If you believe a bedroom should be a restful getaway, then take note. Every detail in this space was carefully planned with just that goal in mind.

An unbelievably fluffy feather topper covers the king bed, which is placed just so for stargazing through the windows. The homeowners have designated the room a tech-free zone; no phones, televisions, or computers are allowed to cross the threshold. But every Sunday, breakfast in bed is served on an antique tray.

Even the chic taupe walls are soothing. Charmingly simple side tables made from local wood are punctuated by petite bell jars repurposed as glass pendants—both of which were designed by the homeowner. And the personal touches continue on the gallery wall, which contains family photos and bits of memorabilia: a visual history, all framed in black and gold.

AUSTIN
Tim Cuppett + Marco Rini
Architect + Garden Designer

**NOT SO BASIC BEDDING.** Tim and Marco have a rule when it comes to top sheets and bottom sheets: they can never match. As a result, they've accumulated a beautiful collection of stripes and floral prints that are mixed at random.

**BUY IT FLOWERS.** Even the most casually thrown-together arrangement is an instant mood lifter. Sprinkle a few stems at the front door, and watch any bad vibes wash away the second you cross the threshold.

# 8 WAYS to love your home so it loves you back

1 **TREAT IT RIGHT.** If you see something that needs attention around the house—a leaky dishwasher, a loose piece of trim—take care of it ASAP. Letting things go in the short term almost always exacerbates the original issue, costing you more money and time in the long run.

2 **BUY IT FLOWERS.** Picking up an inexpensive bunch of flowers (or cutting some from the yard) on a regular basis is a staple of Apartment Therapy's January Cure, our annual guide to starting your year off right. It's a small thing that goes a long way. Colorful blooms can serve as a visual reminder throughout the week that your home—and you!—are worth treating well.

3 **EAT DELICIOUS MEALS TOGETHER.** Whether solo, with family, or for guests, cooking at home is always worth it. Each time you prepare a meal, the benefits increase: your cooking skills sharpen; your kitchen gets more streamlined, because you refine its organization as you use it; and, of course, you get to eat really good home-cooked food.

4 **SERENADE IT.** Turn up the music and belt out a few favorites the next time you're in chores mode; it's way more fun. You can even use the music as a motivator; challenge yourself to finish washing the kitchen floor before the next song starts. You'll clean more energetically and end up happier.

5 **APPRECIATE ITS UNIQUENESS.** No home is perfect. It's the quirks that give it character and charm. Taking the time to turn a challenging spot (a dark entryway, a supersmall bedroom) into an eye-catching design moment is one of the more satisfying projects you can take on—and doing so will make you love your space even more.

6 **DON'T CROWD IT.** Be diligent in letting go of the things you don't need. Your home should be more than a place to store your stuff. Leaving some room to grow is essential to being comfortable in your place, long-term.

7 **DON'T SKIMP ON TIME SPENT TOGETHER.** It's easy to prioritize the time you spend outside your home: working, socializing, exercising. But carving out time on a regular basis to spend an evening in—cooking a meal, taking a long bath—creates a necessary home-life balance. Plus, you'll hit the ground running the next day.

8 **INTRODUCE IT TO YOUR FRIENDS.** Don't keep your wonderful (or on-the-way-to-wonderful) home under wraps. Sharing it with friends, neighbors, and family can inspire you to keep it cleaner, make improvements more often, and simply enjoy it more.

**17**

kids'
spaces

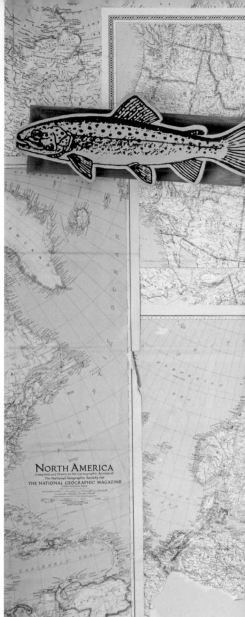

# a bedroom built for three

Epic bed-jumping battles are an everyday occurrence for three growing boys sharing one just-big-enough bedroom. When their family went from three to six in a few short years, these homeowners quickly converted what was once the media room into a camp-themed retreat.

The fun, summer-cabin vibe combines vintage finds with sturdy new pieces in a space that's made for roughhousing. Old maps from *National Geographic* magazines were stuck to the wall with wallpaper paste (and feature a few "hand-drawn" street additions). Camp-y checked curtains flank the windows, and quirky wooden fish trophies hang on the walls.

**SPACE SEPARATION.** (LEFT)
These beds are lined up as close as can be, but smart visual cues—gathered curtains, varied bedding, and stuffed pals—help them appear more distinct.

BARRINGTON, IL
Michelle + Dave Kohanzo
CEO, Land of Nod + Banker
daughter, Emily +
sons Connor, Henry, Everett

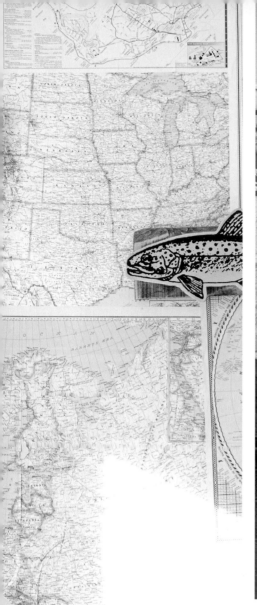

**A DIRECTIONAL PALETTE.**
(CENTER) Covering a whole room in dozens of maps runs the risk of being busy, so Michelle echoed their soft greens, browns, and blues in the rest of the space.

**IN-ROOM ESCAPE HATCH.**
(RIGHT) Sometimes even the most social people need peace and quiet, so tucked behind the half-wall (under the pendant flags) is a tiny reading nook.

A bag of marshmallows (clearly intended for a midnight snack) was even uncovered, stashed behind a row of books on a shelf.

In shared rooms like this, property disputes are the biggest issue, and there's only one surefire solution: give each kid a space of his own. Three equally sized twin beds line the wall (one vintage bed frame and a set of bunk beds that's been split in two). Each boy has a personalized pillow and designated drawer space, as well. "Hey, that's mine," still gets shouted—but, thankfully, not quite as often.

# the pretty-in-pink bedroom

Some girls just really want some bubble-gum pink in their bedrooms—
and this one delivers a whole wall of it. Letting your kids pick the color
of their rooms can be a double-edged sword. On the one hand, it gets
them involved in and excited about the creative design process; on the
other, they could pick chartreuse.

This little girl's bedroom delivered the bright pink pop she wanted,
but it also has a level of restraint and humor. In theory, if you take away
all the pink and pattern, this is a very formal space, balanced with
an ornate headboard centered between two windows. But once you
absorb the single wall of graphic pink scrolling pattern, the whole
room takes on a more playful tone. In lieu of artwork, the Roman shades
feature cartoonish sketches of European street scenes, which work
nicely with the black design in the wallpaper.

You see restraint in the remainder of the room. The rest of the walls
are painted a simple, semigloss white; the floor is covered in neutral
wall-to-wall carpet; and the bedding, too, is white. This keeps the space
from becoming too busy, while an excited little lady gets to decorate her
first "big-girl room."

**STRAIGHT FROM THE FUNNY
PAGES.** (ABOVE) The sketches on
these amazing, graphic shades
are by Saul Steinberg, a famous
cartoonist for *The New Yorker*.
The print, called "Views of Paris,"
dates back to the 1950s.

**A PLACE TO PERCH.** (OPPOSITE)
Original built-in cabinets, which
include a desk and bookshelf,
add some much-needed
functionality to this minimally
furnished room (when they're
not being used as an indoor
jungle gym).

MAPLEWOOD, NJ
Mary + Lou Castelli
Mother + Private Equity Manager
daughter, Sienna + sons Colton, Rex, Bo

**GENIUS AT WORK.** (LEFT) It's a fantastic idea to give kids dedicated space to do their version of "work." As a bonus, this small-scale table and chairs don't take up too much space.

**ROOM TO GROW.** (OPPOSITE) This cheerful room belongs to a small child now, but with a few simple style tweaks—updating the airplane bedding, losing the toys—it could just as easily belong to a teenager.

# the superhero bedroom

This boy's bedroom in Chicago is a collection of all that he holds most dear, including an army of furry little friends and a wall's worth of superhero decals. But his parents have wisely helped curate everything to feel sweet and boyish—and not overly cluttered.

There's a fine line between having *lots* of toys and having an *explosion* of toys. Staying ahead of the chaos when children are constantly falling in love with a new favorite can prove really hard. A good rule of thumb: stick to a strict number of stuffed animals, books, etc., that they're allowed to keep. Getting something new means donating something old. It's a helpful lesson to learn early on.

As a backdrop to all the playtime goodies, the room is painted a soft, light-bouncing blue, which is picked up in the small chairs and cotton rug—pulling everything together a little bit more. And while a dramatic image of Batman rises up over the bed, it is comforting to note that children have many sides, and their rooms show this. They are just as likely to be a superhero in the afternoon as they are to curl up like a baby with a furry yellow duck at bedtime.

CHICAGO
Eric Oliver +
Thea Goodman
Professor + Author
daughter, Esme + son, Ethan

**GROUP SHOW.** (LEFT) Gallery walls visually work as one large piece of art but can be tricky to hang (see chapter 9 for advice). Start by arranging each piece on the floor until you're happy with the overall grouping, then hang it on the wall.

**BABY IKAT.** (OPPOSITE) The super-stylish pink pattern on these curtains is an ikat, which comes from the Malaysian word "mengikat" meaning "to tie." It has the lovely feeling of not being printed but woven from dyed thread.

# the sophisticated nursery

This petite nursery beautifully demonstrates how to successfully pull off a feminine palette and use pink in a way that isn't overly girly.

The pink in question is more of a muted salmon. Layering in soft gray-green walls and an earthy, rusty brown rug helps take the edge off. Strips of yellow (on the curtains, above the crib, and in the artwork) trim the space, further breaking up the girlish moments. A brighter pink, or a pink-and-white-only palette, would not be quite so refined.

Aside from blocking light and absorbing sound, thickly lined black-out curtains lengthen the walls of this tiny room with their strong, vertical pattern. The Moroccan glass light fixture pops with contrast, another grown-up choice, as is the Eames lounger, looking refreshingly out of place as a nursing chair.

Artwork finishes the space. Like the rest of the decor, the collection is a slightly more polished version of what you'd expect to see in a nursery. It's important to remember that in the beginning, you'll be spending just as much time in this room as your little one, so you should pick things you, too, will enjoy looking at.

MILLBURN, NJ
**Jessica + Scott Davis**
Designer, Nest Studio +
Marketing
son, Bryan + daughter, Lucy

# the busy-princess retreat

Every kid needs a place to sleep and a place to play. But all that action can't always be confined to one bedroom—especially in tight New York City apartments. This creative "kid zone" is made of two small connecting spaces: one dedicated to play, another to bedtime.

A custom-made bed is the center of attention in the calm, clutter-free part of the actual bedroom. It was designed to fit perfectly into the narrow space (not a precious inch gets wasted), nestling neatly beneath the window ledge with lots of built-in storage underneath. A gauzy canopy highlights the tall ceiling, while the double headboard makes the colorful nook feel grander than it really is.

Just outside the bedroom is an alcove dedicated to nothing but play. Its "work area" has a place for music, a spot for reading, and arts and crafts projects galore. The kid-height desk takes up an entire wall, meaning she can have multiple projects going at once. Above it sits a stunning vintage mirror. An extra-long row of corkboards acts as a gallery wall for showing off finished work, while the three mounted bookshelves above provide ample storage without taking up precious floor space.

**ORANGE SLICE.** (LEFT) This desk is actually a solid wood IKEA countertop that's been cut to size and covered with three coats of Farrow & Ball high-gloss paint.

**SECOND LIVES.** (ABOVE) The beautiful, arched mirror that grounds this craft nook was once a church window. Maxwell found it at one of his favorite vintage stores, Bobo Intriguing Objects in Atlanta.

**STAND-IN NIGHTSTAND.** (OPPOSITE) In lieu of a side table, which there wasn't space for, a nightlight was mounted to the wall and a wide window shelf was used to hold books.

NEW YORK CITY
Maxwell Ryan
Apartment Therapy Founder
daughter, Ursula

**BOX IT UP.** (LEFT) Literally called "Toy Store," this innovative storage unit from Oeuf tucks neatly in the corner, mimics a store display, and makes pulling out toys (and putting them away) a cinch.

**HAVING A HOOT.** (OPPOSITE) The generous, lively pattern on this bedding and matching curtains is from DwellStudio (the owner's company); the print has been expertly balanced with a double dose of stripes on the sheets and pillowcases.

# the tree-house bedroom

The coziness and creativity of this built-in corner bunk bed is to die for. Designed by the homeowners, it makes great use of a small space, easily expanding from two snoozing residents to four during sleepovers.

Installing a traditional bunk bed here would have wasted a lot of space—and provided plenty of opportunity for books, toys, and clothes to slip down the back of the bed (a.k.a. the land of lost things). This bed is made of common lumber and is attached directly to the wall with built-in safety rails, which double as blanket holders for building epic forts in the bottom bunk.

Lighting is the one major concern with putting a bed this big in a room this small. Bunk beds can overwhelm a space and block light. The many upper windows let in tons of sunlight, while the pastel colors keep things nice and airy. Thanks to all the forest and owl prints, there is a sense of being up in the trees. A sky blue ceiling completes the tree-house theme, and a golden, laser-cut Tord Boontje Tangle Light hangs from the center of the space, providing sparkling "stars" at night.

EAST HAMPTON, NY
Christiane Lemieux +
Joshua Young
Founder, DwellStudio +
Real Estate Developer
daughter, Isabelle + son, William

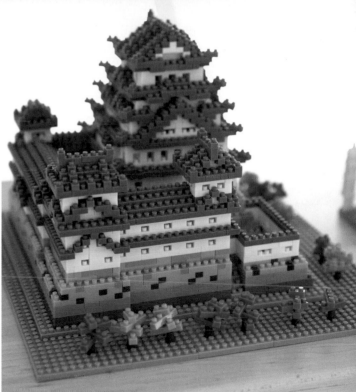

# the lego lair

This sunny, window-walled bedroom is all play, all the time. Every surface is bursting with treasures: amazing LEGO structures, a cello, lots of books, even a flying pirate ship. To make room for this much fun, the owners slid a loft bed/desk combination neatly into a corner, keeping the floor open for the next traffic jam, dragon battle, or castle construction project.

Any parent will tell you that the key to keeping a room this full of toys from slipping into chaos is storage—and this space is full of good-looking solutions. A set of under-the-desk drawers (one for school and art supplies, another for LEGO pieces) keeps the desk clutter-free. Open shelves along the side of the bed hold books and showcase finished projects, and the window wall is lined with big felt bins and an ultralow bench with lots of cubbies. The genius of these low-sitting catchalls is that toys can be dumped out, played with, and put away without your little one ever having to leave the floor.

Remember, a toy tornado can happen in minutes, but if you make putting things away as easy as pulling them out—the damage can be reversed in the same amount of time.

**CLEARLY ORGANIZED.** (LEFT)
See-through storage helps to keep toys visible but neatly tucked away—so "inspector mom" isn't called in every time a favorite plaything goes missing.

**DISPLAY DIORAMAS.** (ABOVE)
As any LEGO-lover can tell you, it takes a while to build these super structures, so having somewhere to admire them is a welcome plus.

**COLOR BLOCKING.** (OPPOSITE)
White walls in a kids' room make sense; their "stuff" is pretty vibrant. But adding some solid swipes of color on top—like these red blinds and purple toy bins—keeps things fun.

CHICAGO
Brenda + David Bergen
Graphic Designer +
Digital Media Consultant
son, Daniel

# her highness's alcove

It's hard to believe, but the dreamy princess retreat you see here used to be a boring old laundry room. It was transformed with a custom mattress (shorter than a twin) and an immense canopy that envelops the whole thing.

This is a nice example of working a very large-scale object into a very small-scale room. The effect is wildly luxurious despite the limited space. What you see here is the whole shebang: a bed, a small dresser, and a lamp. There's no extra square footage hiding off camera. As a result, this one amazing element becomes the big event.

When you dissect it, the canopy is simply thick, upholstered valances attached to the ceiling and heavy curtains that hang to the floor. From the outside, the fabric is solid pink, but inside, layered patterns draw you in, emphasizing the intimacy of the tiny tentlike bed.

While this is a richly done faux four-poster bed in a window, you can create something similar on any budget. The main detail to get right: attach your canopy and curtains to the ceiling (or walls) so that they fill the space and seem like a continuation of the mattress below.

LOS ANGELES
**Ruthie Sommers +**
**Luke McDonough**
Interior Designer + CEO, AirMedia
daughters Eloise, Bailey, Posey

EAST HAMPTON, NY
Christiane Lemieux + Joshua Young
Founder, DwellStudio + Real Estate Developer
daughter, Isabelle + son, William

**18**

bathrooms

# the indoor/outdoor bathroom

Welcome to the ultimate beach house bathroom. The outdoor shower is constructed entirely of reclaimed salvage materials. Multiple old doors and windows define the structure itself, but the truly surprising detail is its gorgeous greenery. Nature has been allowed to squirm its way into this space, resulting in a wonderful, rain-forest feeling.

Located two quick steps from the rest of the house via a private side entrance, the shower area has a durable tile floor (meant to stand up to sandy, post-beach rinse-offs) and a slight overhang that keeps the sink portion of the room out of the weather. An extra-large showerhead, mostly hidden by leaves, hangs in the center.

A private wash closet, with a striking vintage "throne," is connected to the main house. Thriving greenery has found its way into this space, as well, with tight clusters of vines climbing the cinder-block wall.

Nothing about these rooms is precious, and the lack of pristine white surfaces offers a sense of freedom—as if you're forever on vacation. Most people don't have the luxury of an outdoor shower, but bringing a little bit of greenery (maybe a succulent or two) into your own bathroom can give you a taste of this jungle-y goodness.

VENICE BEACH
Susan + Kevin Lennon
Owner, SHOP by h. bleu +
Founder, Lennon Design
daughter, Griffin

**SINGING IN THE RAIN (SHOWER).** (OPPOSITE) When this small guesthouse was being built, the idea of keeping the shower separate from the main house was a huge breakthrough. Not only are the results magical, it was also a far more wallet-friendly construction.

**PRIVATE SEAT.** (ABOVE) Hidden behind a frosted-glass door, this vintage green toilet bridges the main water closet with the shower outside.

**PAINT IT BLACK.** (LEFT) Vintage claw-foot tubs are not hard to find, but they are often in poor shape. Don't get discouraged; reglazing the interior and painting the outside is a simple enough update.

**RETRO TILE.** (OPPOSITE) After decades of use, the tile in this bathroom was due for a renovation. In keeping with the historic nature of the house, the owner installed a classic "octagon and dot" pattern.

# the art deco bathroom

This petite master bathroom is full of built-in vintage charm. It's crisp and bright, with lots of black and white details and a just-right mix of old versus new.

A bathroom is the one room where "worn-in" details aren't necessarily charming. So when mixing in vintage pieces, it's important to think about how they will hold up. Here, the original built-in wall storage from the '30s is extremely cool and functional. New hardware and the occasional coat of paint help to hide its age. The claw-foot tub, also vintage, will last for decades with regular cleaning. And a beautiful Art Deco mirror, hung above the toilet, sets the mood for the whole space.

The new elements complement the old ones perfectly—a retro mirror wastebasket and a beautifully detailed sink. Like the claw feet of the tub, the pedestal base of the sink, with its delicate body, adds a certain airiness to the heavier pieces. When you want to visually expand a space, lighter feet and a lift off the floor will always make a difference.

LOS ANGELES
Laura Jay Freedman
Shop Owner, Broken English

# the dark spa retreat

Dark colors are the "comfort food" of decorating, and in this master bathroom, they look both indulgent and fascinating.

Typically, you want to expand a small space through light colors, and only use darker shades in the lower portion of a room (if at all). Deep colors can add a nice, strong contrast to a space, but they can also visually contract it.

This room reverses the norm with absolutely stunning results. Bright white tile bounces natural light through the space from below. But up above, contemporary toile wallpaper and a chocolate-brown coved ceiling create a refreshingly warm, intimate, and comfortable atmosphere. Beautiful dark wood antiques, including an intricately carved mirror, glass-front cabinet, and dresser-turned-vanity, add to the formality of this type of design.

The mix feels very Old World, not unlike an apothecary shop, with small, feminine touches sprinkled about: neatly organized beauty products on trays, fresh flowers, and black-and-white framed photographs. This kind of dark, romantic retreat can only be achieved by taking every rule you've ever learned about color and throwing it out the window.

**BUREAU REVIVAL. (ABOVE)** This ornate wood sideboard was nearing the end of its life when it was smartly turned into a grand sink with a marble top.

**SUNKEN TUB. (OPPOSITE)** Wanting a large, modern tub for soaking that didn't break from their traditional style, the owners skillfully wrapped this one with stained wood panels that match the sideboard-turned-sink.

LOS ANGELES
Lulu Powers +
Stephen Danelian
The Entertainologist +
Founder, MeeLocal

**PALE BLUE PLANKS.** (LEFT) This is the only painted floor in the entire house; the soft shade is reminiscent of eighteenth-century European or Shaker floors. Adding a glossy finish helps combat the post-shower dampness.

**SHELF LIFE.** (OPPOSITE) Above pedestal sinks, a simple glass shelf mounted on the wall at any height is an unexpectedly chic alternative to the traditional medicine cabinet.

# the breezy beach house bathroom

This lovely, pared-down, rustic style is dependent on four things: clean, almost white walls; carefully considered Old World details; a love of symmetry; and a subtle splash of color.

In this spacious bathroom the most notable feature is the pretty sky blue floor—a soft shade washed over antique pine planks. Other than this, there is very little adornment. With empty walls and only one piece of artwork, your attention is drawn to the lovely fittings and materials.

Modern, wall-mounted towel rods were eschewed for vintage swinging bars instead; over-the-sink mirrors skipped in favor of a collection of smaller antique ones. And, in the hardest-working part, a bank of storage cabinets replaces the need for a linen closet. Towels are stacked and left out; a separate open bank (not pictured) holds daily-use beauty supplies; while everything else is hidden behind two shutterlike doors. All together, the cabinets create a nice, balanced rhythm in the room.

When you concentrate less on making a major style moment, the small details of your space can sing.

EAST COAST
Deborah Nevins
Landscape Designer

# the *old man and the sea* bathroom

The longest wall in this alleyway-of-a-rental-bathroom is covered in framed nautical-themed photos that include scary-movie sea creatures, black-and-white fishing scenes, and images of Ernest Hemingway. A well-curated gallery wall sets the tone for the whole "salty sailor" vibe in the space, and though it *looks* like an expensive art collection, the truth is . . . it isn't.

All these images were found online, printed on nice paper, and mounted in white IKEA frames. When you're just starting out, and artwork is a luxury beyond your means, this is a smart, crafty way to mimic the look (until you can slowly start to buy and sprinkle in the real thing).

On the opposite side of the room, the nautical theme picks back up: a picture of an old ship hangs over the sink, echoing a similar image on a coaster that sits with other sea-themed tchotchkes on the toilet tank. A fun but loose theme like this is a nice way to make a big impact in a small room. One note of warning, though: don't let yourself get too carried away (a life-size mermaid shower curtain would definitely cross the line).

**TANK TOP.** (LEFT) It can be a challenge to make a display of objects (even pretty objects) on top of a porcelain tank feel purposeful. Using a tray frames the collection and keeps things from slipping off.

**IN BLACK & WHITE.** (ABOVE) While she could have used black frames, this homeowner chose a wide, white style; a much more dramatic contrast against the deep charcoal walls.

**LIGHT SHOW.** (OPPOSITE) Painting a small room a dark shade is risky, but Taylor made smart use of the window above the bathtub by hanging a white shower liner that defuses light through the space.

BROOKLYN
Taylor Swaim
Brand Creative

**SQUEAKY CLEAN.** (LEFT) With four small children in the house, this galley bathroom sees a lot of daily use. Double sinks and a large soaker tub mean multiple little ones can get ready for bed at once.

**TAKE IT UP A NOTCH.** (OPPOSITE) Dutch designer Dick van Hoff created this cool, modern mirror. It slides and locks onto two wall-mounted knobs for an effect that's both retro and fun.

# the modern '80s bathroom

Clean, gridded spaces in simple, bright colors were a hallmark of 1980s design. Now that the decade is thirty-five years in our rearview mirror, there is something fresh and appealing about the cheerfulness and optimism it brought.

The two bathrooms you see here—one a main-floor powder room, the other a heavily used kids' washroom—both offer perfect examples. Each uses one bright color as an accent, either on the floor or wall, while the rest of the room stays white, so as not to compete.

A simple, one-color palette can run the risk of falling flat. But here, the family avoided that pitfall by injecting color through small tiles, which contribute lots of gridded texture to the space—a treatment that makes the saturated shades come alive.

A fascinating interplay also results from the tiles' neat, straight lines and the curvy bathroom fixtures. All the toilets in this house are very slim, round Toto models. The sinks have modern, exaggerated, circular designs. And the lighting in the kids' bathroom seems to drip from the ceiling like water. These moments offer contrast and depth in the happy-go-lucky rooms.

MAPLEWOOD, NJ
Mary + Lou Castelli
Mother + Private Equity Manager
daughter, Sienna + sons Colton, Rex, Bo

SPA BATH. (LEFT) In order to keep the big, deep soaking tub from visually taking over the whole bathroom, the platform surround was stained to match the flooring, and the white siding was painted the same shade as the window trim.

SHIMMERING GLASS. (OPPOSITE) Tiles can add stunning color and pattern to a bathroom, but glass tiles are particularly good at capturing and showing off the light.

# the zen garden retreat

Showers are practical, but tubs are luxurious. Great bathrooms have both—and, ideally, not in the same footprint. This master bath has a deep soaking tub and a stunning shower with enough room to sit down, and is drenched with sunlight for most of the day.

Built along one full wall, the tub is surrounded by windows on three sides. An exposed ceiling beam visually separates it from the rest of the space, giving the illusion of a smaller, more intimate setting. The cast-iron bath sits in a wood frame, which provides plenty of extra surface space for towels, soaps, flowers, even artwork. Adding a platform like this doesn't require a lot of work or money, but the end result is definitely luxurious.

Designed with three shades of green glass tiles, the mood of the shower is completely different. An extra-large skylight in the ceiling makes you feel that you're in an outdoor shower. Large potted plants and a black floor made of polished stones complete the illusion that you're standing outside in a warm rain.

VENICE BEACH
**Susan + Kevin Lennon**
Owner, SHOP by h. bleu +
Founder, Lennon Design
daughter, Griffin

**LOW-SITTING LIGHTS.** Not only has this homeowner used a smartly placed floor lamp to "exaggerate" the size of her small living room, she also upped the results by adding an over-the-fireplace fixture that focuses light—and therefore attention—on the lower half of the space.

# 8 WAYS to make a small room look bigger

1 **LOW-SITTING LIGHTS.** Keep overhead lights off; use floor and table lamps instead. This illuminates the lower half of the room. It's a simple trick that makes ceilings seem higher and rooms airier.

2 **BIG-ENOUGH RUGS.** In a small living room, one large rug that all your furniture can sit on will make your space feel cohesive, less broken up. When pieces float outside the perimeter, they create chaos– the opposite of what you want in a room, but especially detrimental in a small space.

3 **MEANDERING FLOW.** Never sacrifice flow Easy access in and out of a room is far more important than adding "one more piece." Awkward, cut-off movement between spaces can make any size room feel small, so check that your layout gives you more than one way to enter and exit the main areas of your home. (For more tips on good flow, see chapter 2.)

4 **EMPTY SPACE.** When square footage is at a premium, it can feel like a necessity to fill every last inch. But the price for packing those surfaces is a room that looks even smaller. Leaving some open space sends a visual message that there is room to spare. The things you do display will pack an even greater style punch.

5 **PERFECT PAIRS.** Buy in double: matching floor lamps or two small love seats instead of a sofa and two chairs. The cohesiveness adds balance to tight spaces and reduces the impression of clutter—which can sneak up on you when you're juggling scale, color, and multiple finishes in one room.

6 **BIG, BEAUTIFUL, BOLD ART.** Gallery walls are great (and definitely work in a small space), but sticking with one or two oversize pieces instead can boost the appearance of a room's size. Big art in a small space creates a scale differential that is always visually interesting. Rather than dwarfing the space, it tends to expand it.

7 **MINIMALIST LIVING.** Fact: small rooms look more spacious when you have a few pieces of large furniture—rather than a whole lot of small furniture. The reason? Less visual noise and an uncomplicated floor plan, which (as we've already mentioned) is essential for good flow.

8 **EXTRA-WIDE WINDOW TREATMENTS.** Whenever possible, extend your curtain rod out beyond the width of the window frame. It's a bit of an optical illusion that makes windows seem larger, which, in turn, makes rooms feel more spacious.

**19**

outdoor
spaces

**MOSAIC MEALS.** (LEFT) Great outdoors and easy to clean, this glass-tile-topped table is the homeowners' own design and comes in fifteen different shades, providing a great opportunity to add color where most folks choose a neutral wood.

**RAW MATERIALS.** (OPPOSITE) The pinkish-red hue of the dividing wall comes from pigmented (not painted) concrete, meaning the color is stirred right into the cement mix. The walls will age gracefully, revealing beautiful new tones the more weathered they get.

# the plant whisperer's wonderland

What started as a small slice of land in LA's Elysian Park neighborhood has evolved, over decades, into the stunning half-acre property you see here. The green thumb behind this lush sanctuary is professional landscape designer Judy Kameon, who purchased adjoining lots through the years and turned them into an extended garden.

At the epicenter of it all is an ancient pepper tree that rivals the size of the house. An oval patio covered in decomposed granite circles its trunk and is the go-to destination for meals of all sizes; the table seats ten easily.

The curving frame of this platform sets the direction for the rest of the garden. Rather than work in rectangles (the norm), every section of the sloping yard reflects an interlocking set of curves. Low-growing greenery lines the major divides, building to larger, more dramatic plants the deeper each bed gets.

The lozenge-shaped pool nestles into the curves perfectly. Note the mottled red and blue tones in the retaining wall and pool bottom, a mirror of the plants that surround them.

If a fluid garden is your goal, think about mimicking the curving flow you see here. It's a less formal approach that allows you to slowly expand your garden over time.

LOS ANGELES
Judy Kameon +
Erik Otsea
Landscape Designer +
Outdoor Furniture Designer
son, Ian

# the family deck

One of the many great things about living in Southern California? Glorious outdoor spaces like this can be enjoyed year-round. The big backyard deck is a destination for family meals, group homework sessions, and plain old relaxing.

The patio is made from recycled-plastic decking, which lasts longer and requires less upkeep than wood. But the handy homeowners assembled everything else that brings this retreat to life from salvage and flea market finds.

Temporarily covered by a plastic roof (until the homeowners pick a more permanent solution), the L-shaped lounge area is actually just wood shipping pallets topped with cushions and throw pillows. Extra-deep seating invites sitting, reclining, or napping, and small outdoor lights provide a soft glow for after-dinner conversations that stretch into the night.

At the opposite end of the deck, directly outside the kitchen, a long reclaimed-wood table seats a dozen—and when it needs a good cleaning, it's tough enough to be hosed down. If only all big cleanups were that easy.

**LOOK AT THAT FACE!** (LEFT) This heavy-duty cotton duck fabric (originally used to make vintage mail and military bags) not only stands up to wetness, it's pet-friendly too.

**PLANT COVER.** (ABOVE) Stacked at various heights, an assortment of planters (all old street lampposts that were turned into flowerpots) hide the not-so-pretty underside of the deck's sitting area.

**COMFY CORNER.** (OPPOSITE) Part of the L-shaped nook is currently topped with a few pieces of fiberglass. It allows plenty of light to pass through, so a thick and fragrant vine can continue to grow in the space.

VENICE BEACH
Susan + Kevin Lennon
Owner, SHOP by h. bleu +
Founder, Lennon Design
daughter, Griffin

**ALFRESCO DINING.** For this large family, having a full kitchen outside the house is an essential pleasure. There's a large grill, refrigerator, and makeshift sideboard that doubles as a buffet and storage.

# the nature observatory

Located a few hours from the craziness of Manhattan, this weekend retreat is surrounded by nature. The screened in porch overlooks a shallow pond. You can watch fish jumping in the morning, snapping turtles dozing in the afternoon, and dozens of species of birds flitting around at dusk.

With such a thriving ecosystem to preserve, the homeowners were careful to create outdoor spaces for observing but not disrupting the wild-life. To separate the front yard from the wetlands, a mulch path and hand-laid stone wall were put in. But despite the lawn's many lounge chairs, everyone ends up on the dark, cozy porch.

For an outdoor space, this porch has all the comforts of indoors. A high-backed armchair is upholstered in a furry vintage fabric. To lighten the palette, an animal skin rug was layered in, while pops of red call attention to the window seat.

Bringing inside furniture outdoors makes a very luxe statement. But there are a few rules to follow: select durable fabrics, clean everything frequently, and avoid leaving upholstered pieces in direct sunlight, which fades fabric and disinte-grates cushion stuffing.

ELIZAVILLE, NY
Christopher Coleman  + Angel Sanchez
Interior Designer + Fashion Designer

**LEAN INTO IT.** Instead of a basic, square-shaped screen porch, this one has a long wall set at a slight angle, which makes the closed-off room feel more open.

# the chauffeur's garden estate

Tucked behind a row of manicured hedges in LA's Hancock Park, these elegant outdoor spaces belong to the carriage house of what was once a much larger estate. The home and gardens have long since been separated from their original parent next door, but the overall mood is no less grand. All the outdoor areas are luxurious destinations. But, more than that, they are a boon of extra space for a house that may look palatial but actually has a relatively small footprint for a family of five.

With its perfect symmetry, tall cypress trees, and multiple pavilions, the pool is very old Hollywood, like a scene from a Slim Aarons photograph come to life. However, all that formality doesn't keep an army of little ones (and a dog who loves to swim) out of this pool.

In the shadiest corner of the property, a brick courtyard is the scene of low-key meals and afternoon naps in the hammock. A hefty marble table might not seem like an obvious choice for outside, but it's extremely durable—and will outlive typical outdoor furniture. In a truly handy design move, the seat *and* cushions pop right out of these chairs, so you can store them when they're not in use.

**TWIN PAVILIONS.** (ABOVE)
The pool is flanked by two grand, identically constructed pavilions—one formally decorated, the other (not pictured) more low-key and playful.

**ONE LUMP OR TWO?** (OPPOSITE)
This newly installed, open patio is the perfect scene for kid-friendly, adult-size tea parties with its pale bricks (laid in a formal herringbone pattern), marble-top dining table, and pillow-filled hammock.

LOS ANGELES
**Ruthie Sommers +
Luke McDonough**
Interior Designer + CEO, AirMedia
daughters Eloise, Bailey, Posey

**OLD STYLE.** Nestled right up against the house, the shape of the pool mixes beautifully with the flat, white facade and deep green trees. It feels more like a water feature than a kid's playground (though technically it's both).

**FOLLOW THE FOLIAGE.** (LEFT)
Instead of overcrowding the sitting area, Laura tucked her grill away at the far end of the long walkway next to her house.

**SMALL FOOTPRINTS.** (OPPOSITE)
The selection of greenery planted here is smart on two fronts: it's easy to care for, yes, but each plant was also selected for its small trunk and large leaves, which make the garden feel more lush

# a sunny scrap of patio

Ask apartment dwellers what luxury item is at the top of their wish list for their next home, and nine out of ten people will tell you it's an outdoor space. Having access to a garden, deck, or even a fire escape with potted plants goes a long way toward your overall happiness.

This small patio is a great example of making the most of what you have. Like many LA homes, it's perched on the side of a hill; other places crowd it from all sides. But this scrap of concrete has been turned into a lush oasis with minimal effort.

Low-sitting Acapulco chairs and a round metal table set the tone for this retro hangout. Greenery positively explodes over the retaining wall, where low-maintenance plants, including young palm trees that will eventually grow high enough to give the patio more shade and privacy, fill the raised garden. To bring a little bit of that greenery down to eye level, potted plants line the pathway along the side of the house.

Spending any amount of time creating an outdoor space of your own (even if that means a window-box herb garden) will always be worth the effort.

LOS ANGELES
Laura Jay Freedman
Shop Owner, Broken English

# the texas-style front porch

This idyllic farmhouse is straight out of a movie. Rows of Knock Out Roses and fields of bluebonnets (the state flower of Texas) surround it. The wraparound front porch, rocking chair, and zigzagging strings of globe lights feel like a charming, 1950s version of classic Americana. But the truth is, this home is actually a fairly new construction (built in 1997).

All the hard-sought vintage details (brought back to life by the handy homeowners) establish the old-timey mood. In the front yard, a weathered wood swing hangs from a large live oak tree. The covered porch is laced with scalloped wood beams above and framed by a proper whitewashed railing along the side. And a soft, pale palette gives everything a sun-bleached look.

Sturdy and not precious at all, the lovingly collected furniture—mostly locally sourced antiques—makes perfect sense in a high-traffic, kid-frequented zone like this. A few flour-sack throw pillows keep things cozy during extended games of checkers, and the collection of folding red bistro chairs offers more space for the party to grow as neighbors swing by.

**GAME NIGHT.** (LEFT) Antique carrom boards, like this one from the 1960s, are modern collectibles. Aside from their graphic artistry, they accommodate upward of fifty games, from chess to table shuffleboard.

**HOUSEWARMING GIFT.** (ABOVE) This tree swing has been hanging here since long before the Hulls moved in. The couple fell in love with it immediately, heart-shaped carvings and all.

**INTO THE FOLD.** (OPPOSITE) Every piece of outdoor furniture on this porch collapses and folds, making it easier to stow in the winter months.

ROUND TOP, TEXAS
Paige + Smoot Hull
Bed & Breakfast Owners
son, Pierce + daughters Eisley, Cameron

**DAY BED.** (LEFT) A simple army cot is turned into a far more luxurious destination when topped with a soft, down-filled, linen "throwbed" by Hedgehouse. The look could be very "princess in the pea" if you were to stack multiple beds on top of one another.

**ALL WRAPPED UP.** (OPPOSITE) Ever the gracious host, Anne thinks of even the smallest details. Affordable cashmere blankets from West Elm are draped over the chairs for the moment the chilly night air sweeps in.

# an alfresco dining spot in the hills

Cut into the steep hillside of Laurel Canyon, this petite outdoor space feels as though it could just as easily overlook Italy's Amalfi Coast. The tangle of greenery and winding gravel paths zigzag the property (like the walkways of a small European village), each dead-ending in its own little oasis.

The dining area is an inviting mix of beach-y furniture (a wood-slat table and chairs topped with a canvas umbrella) and simple, sophisticated accents (cashmere blankets, glass lanterns, and a very Mediterranean blue and white tablescape). Above this landing, up a steep set of stairs, there's a grassy knoll for stargazing; next to it, a vintage military cot, the go-to destination for impromptu naps.

This multilevel property is a work in progress. Landslides (on a small scale) are a frequent occurrence. The new homeowners combated this naturally by embedding large stones into the steep dirt wall and surrounding them with deep-rooted plants to help retain the soil—a very visually pleasing landscaping approach. An herb garden is in the works, but for now, easy-to-care-for potted plants line the side of the house, extending the feeling of a lush green oasis.

LOS ANGELES
Anne Ziegler +
Scott Mason
Trend Forecaster +
Entertainment Executive

# the easy english garden

When a Southern architect and an Oxford-trained garden designer plan an outdoor space together, you can count on two things: there will be plenty of room for entertaining and plenty of eye candy to explore. This home's charm begins at the front gate, where wildflowers line a white picket fence, and an enormous swing hangs from a pecan tree.

In the backyard, symmetrical garden beds are trimmed with manicured boxwood bushes; they contain vegetables, herbs, and flowering accents, including a Peggy Martin climbing rosebush. Tall Japanese blueberry trees provide tons of essential shade.

In the background, the shed holds supplies and keeps the compost station out of sight. A shingle-clad cistern collects rainwater for watering the yard—a system that isn't expensive to install and will save you tons on water bills. And one of the true (almost forgotten) treats of having a yard: a clothesline hangs just outside the laundry room window.

AUSTIN
Tim Cuppett + Marco Rini
Architect + Garden Designer

**KNOW YOUR HISTORY.** The key to a flourishing garden, according to Marco (the master behind this yard), is listening to longtime residents and finding out what works well. Forcing unlikely-to-succeed plants to grow is fodder for frustration.

# the urban jungle

Located right off a busy city street, behind an unassuming front gate, this home is surrounded by so much greenery that the rest of the world seems miles away.

A brick path greets you at the entrance, leading you through the multiple outdoor spaces sprinkled around the property. Rather than forming a straight line from point A to point B, the walkway has a gentle meander to it, which fits right in with the unhurried, "time doesn't matter here" mood of the whole space. At its end, a little backyard opens onto a small tile patio (just off the master bedroom), a

ROYAL TENT. (LEFT) This striking sitting area is a glamorous mix of indoor and outdoor furniture, all framed in a boldly striped canvas pavilion with curtain walls.

LOS ANGELES
Lulu Powers + Stephen Danelian
The Entertainologist + Founder, MeeLocal

**BRICK-BY-BRICK.** (CENTER) To emphasize the subtle twist in this pathway, the center pavers were laid horizontally and framed by three rows of vertically placed bricks.

**SUN PATIO.** (RIGHT) The owners opened up an exterior wall to connect the bedroom to their yard, adding elegant French doors and steps that are now home to dozens of potted plants.

hot tub that doubles as a fountain, and a dramatic striped gazebo for entertaining.

Central to the style here is the multiplicity of plants, both potted and not. Vines have overtaken the walls of the home, while ground cover and colorful planters outline the property and fill the steps. A joyfulness comes from living with all this healthy greenery, and it is important that there is no formality to it. A collection of eclectic and hardy plants in varying shapes and sizes gives off a casualness that is accessible—and easy to duplicate.

CHICAGO
Lisa + Joel Santos
Gourmet Grocer/Chef +
Computer Developer

# maintaining your home

the year-round healthy &
happy home calendar

## january

○ **CLEAN:** Join the January Cure on Apartment Therapy, a kickoff to a cleaner, more organized home for the year ahead.

○ **MAINTAIN:** Flip your mattress, and while you're at it, vacuum up those under-the-bed dust bunnies and launder your pillows (check the label for instructions).

○ **LET GO:** As you put away your holiday decor, pull out the items you didn't use, and donate or swap them with friends.

○ **DECORATE:** Shop the annual white sales for towels and bedding. Now's the time to stock up.

○ **ENJOY:** Host a get-together at the end of the month to celebrate your newly "cured" home.

## february

○ **CLEAN:** Give all the lighting in your house a good wipe-down; dust the bases, bulbs, globes, and fixtures. Gently brush or vacuum the shades, too.

○ **MAINTAIN:** Check that your disaster supplies are in good standing. Replace items as needed. (Visit Ready.gov for a full list of recommended supplies.)

○ **LET GO:** Spend an hour trying on your special-occasion and work clothes. Pass things on that don't fit—or anything you'll never wear—to friends or a local charity.

○ **DECORATE:** This is a good month to find deals on floor coverings and furniture, as shops make room for new spring styles.

○ **ENJOY:** A special, splurge-y dinner prepared with gourmet ingredients (for one or more) is the perfect treat for this still-wintry month.

## march

○ **CLEAN:** Wash your walls—yes, they need cleaning, too. Dust, then wipe the surface with a damp sponge, paying special attention to baseboards. (If you have flat paint, make sure the sponge is barely wet to avoid water stains.) Clean smudges and scuffs with a gentle all-purpose cleaner.

○ **MAINTAIN:** Change the batteries in your smoke alarm and carbon monoxide detector. If you have a fireplace, get the chimney cleaned and inspected.

○ **LET GO:** Gather books and magazines you've already read and find places to pass them on to: a senior center, shelter, or hospital.

○ **DECORATE:** The little things you use every day are so important. For a small but mighty lift, choose one of the following that feels extra-tired and replace it:
  • Kitchen cabinet hardware
  • Light-switch plates
  • Bath mats and shower curtains
  • Place mats, napkins, or tablecloth
  • A small appliance: hair dryer, coffeemaker, or iron, for instance

○ **ENJOY:** Make it a priority to play music at home. Find time to discover new artists, or play old favorites (while cooking on Sunday mornings is a great starting point).

### the YEAR-ROUND healthy & happy home calendar

Truly loving your home means taking care of it. Just like anything worth doing, it requires some effort. But sprinkling your energy throughout the year, getting lots of good stuff done at a natural, sensible, seasonal pace will keep things manageable. Build in ways to let stuff go. Enjoy spending time at home. And remind yourself to slow down, worry less, and live a little lighter and happier. Every month, pop these five things onto your to-do list for a well-rounded, low-stress way to keep your home relaxation-ready.

# april

○ **CLEAN:** Thoroughly wipe ceiling fans. Then set their direction to counterclockwise (if they aren't already) to produce a breeze and help cool your home.

○ **MAINTAIN:** Dry-clean or launder cold-weather bedding. Pack it away for next season.

○ **LET GO:** Flip your closet. Clean and put away winter clothes. Donate or swap the ones you haven't worn at all this season. And as you unpack your warm-weather clothes, edit them, adding things you know you won't wear to the donation out-box.

○ **DECORATE:** Spruce up your front door. If you're a homeowner, consider painting the door a splashy new color. If you rent, try adding a garden container or a fun new welcome mat.

○ **ENJOY:** Kick spring off right with a serious self-care weekend—or week! Make it a priority to eat well, sleep in, get a haircut, or book a massage or facial.

# may

○ **CLEAN:** Start some good daily habits. Complete these three tasks every single day, no exceptions, for the entire month:

- Make the bed first thing in the morning
- De-clutter all surfaces as you go about your day (instead of letting them pile up)
- Complete kitchen cleanup before going to bed

○ **MAINTAIN:** On the first really warm day, open the windows, turn on the fans, and air out your whole place. Good-bye, stale air! Hello, spring!

○ **LET GO:** Clear out those mismatched glasses, straggler utensils, and old dishes. Fewer "extras" equal less-crowded cabinets, which is never a bad thing.

○ **DECORATE:** Get going on your outdoor space. Make sure you have what you need for seating, cooking, and entertaining. If something didn't survive last summer in good condition, replace it now.

○ **ENJOY:** Take up something creative you've always wanted to try: photography, knitting, baking, writing, or upholstery. Extra credit for finishing your first project over the summer!

# june

○ **CLEAN:** Do a massive refrigerator clean-out: remove everything, wipe the fridge down (inside and out), and vacuum the coils to keep the cooling at its most efficient. Restock in an organized way, tossing anything that has expired.

○ **MAINTAIN:** Whip your bathroom into shape. Take a few hours, and really scrub. Clean out your cabinets, wash the floor, and deep-clean the tub, toilet, and sink. Get that tile gleaming!

○ **LET GO:** Lighten your key ring's load. Remove keys you no longer regularly use. Put them in an envelope, and mark the date and what they're for on the front. If you need them, you know where they are. But if, in a year (when you do this again), you haven't touched them, toss them.

○ **DECORATE:** Simplify for summer. Try storing heavy throws and area rugs and letting your rooms go a bit bare for the season. Bonus: things will feel "new" again when you bring them back into the mix come fall.

○ **ENJOY:** Be the nice neighbor. Turn an acquaintance into a friend by extending an invitation for a casual meal.

# july

○ **CLEAN:** Give upholstered furniture a refresh. Take pillows and cushions outside for a thorough dusting and airing out. Wipe down the hard surfaces, and vacuum the upholstered sections, using the correct attachments.

○ **MAINTAIN:** It's been six months . . . time to flip the mattress. And don't forget: vacuum those dust bunnies, and launder your pillows again.

○ **LET GO:** You loved them when you bought them, but it's time to surrender some of your shoes. Get rid of any pairs that fall into the following categories: You can't walk in them for more than fifteen minutes. They don't *actually* match that green dress you bought them for. They're so well loved, they're worn out (even your cobbler says they're hopeless).

○ **DECORATE:** 'Tis the season for garage sales and flea markets. Make a point of going treasure hunting at least once in the hope of adding some vintage goodness to your place.

○ **ENJOY:** As a reward for letting go of some of your shoes, strap on your comfiest (remaining) pair, and enjoy a long walk, with an ice cream parlor as your destination.

# august

○ **CLEAN:** Focus on your floors. Wash or dry-clean small rugs. Have larger rugs or wall-to-wall carpeting professionally cleaned. And while the rugs are at the cleaners, take the opportunity to polish or wax your hardwood floors.

○ **MAINTAIN:** Review your household paperwork. Make sure all records, warranties, and policies are up-to-date. Get rid of those you no longer need, and extend any that are nearing expiration.

○ **LET GO:** You've got a month. Set aside your newer products and finish up (or clear out) all those almost-empty shampoos, conditioners, and makeup. Keep in mind that items like mascara, liquid eyeliner, anti-aging creams, and acne treatments expire after three months.

○ **DECORATE:** Join the Style Cure on Apartment Therapy, and spruce up one room in your house.

○ **ENJOY:** Before life gets busier—and the weather gets colder—spend some time exploring your neighborhood's new local businesses. A big part of loving your home is knowing and supporting the good people around it.

# september

○ **CLEAN:** Show your window treatments some attention. Dry-clean or launder curtains. Dust or vacuum fabric shades. Wipe down venetian blinds and shutters.

○ **MAINTAIN:** Check the batteries in your smoke alarm and carbon monoxide detector again. (It's been six months already!) Get your heating/cooling system inspected and cleaned.

○ **LET GO:** Sort through your toys and games. Box up any your family no longer uses (but that are still in good condition) to donate to a shelter or after-school program.

○ **DECORATE:** Got the bedroom blahs? A refreshed look is one colorful new throw blanket or a few pretty pillowcases away. For a bigger impact, add new bedside lighting or switch out your artwork.

○ **ENJOY:** Make a complete, start-to-finish, new-to-you meal—from appetizer to dessert. Take the opportunity to try a new wine (or two), as well! If you decide to invite guests, embrace the experiment, and let them weigh in on the menu when they RSVP.

# october

○ **CLEAN:** Dedicate some time to your ceiling fans—again. Wipe down the blades, and reverse their direction to clockwise—which pulls up cool air and pushes down warm air—to help heat your home.

○ **MAINTAIN:** Remove and clean all air vents, heat registers, and exhaust fans. It will up the air quality in your home during the months ahead, when the windows stay shut more often.

○ **LET GO:** Flip your closet for fall. Pack away your warm-weather clothes. Swap or donate the things you haven't worn this season. And as you unpack your cold-weather items, put anything you no longer want in the donation out-box.

○ **DECORATE:** "Cozify" your home for the months and holidays ahead. Switch out a few key accessories, curtains, and throws; embrace different textures, colors, and scents that celebrate the seasonal shift.

○ **ENJOY:** Become an amateur mixologist. Teach yourself to make a new cocktail to enjoy (and serve) over the next few months.

# november

○ **CLEAN:** Clean the things that clean. Give your dishwasher, washing machine, and vacuum cleaner some much-earned attention. Wipe the exteriors and attachments. Add a cup of white vinegar to your washing machine and dishwasher, and let them run through a full cycle. Change the HEPA filter in your vacuum cleaner, if it has one.

○ **MAINTAIN:** After Thanksgiving, check that your stove and oven survived the chaos. Soak the burner grates, knobs, and oven racks in warm, soapy water. Scrub the stovetop with a surface cleaner. If you have a self-cleaning oven, turn on the cleaning cycle. If not, consult the cleaning instructions.

○ **LET GO:** Reflect a bit on your good fortune, and then give a little of your time, money, or expertise to an organization that needs it.

○ **DECORATE:** Stay ahead of winter pileups by prepping your entryway with a good solution for hats, gloves, and other accessories, plus ample tray space for dirty shoes and boots.

○ **ENJOY:** Eat a piece of pie for breakfast the day after Thanksgiving, even if that means going out and buying a pie to make it happen.

# december

○ **CLEAN:** De-clutter your media center: organize movies, dust all the components, and adjust wires to hide as many as possible.

○ **MAINTAIN:** Make sure all holiday lights and decorations are in good working order before using them. If in doubt, toss them—it's not worth the risk.

○ **LET GO:** Give yourself a break. Let go of any expectations of perfection that can crop up during the holiday season. Accept the realities of time and budget constraints—and simply enjoy.

○ **DECORATE:** Go big . . . or not! Set a deadline for getting your decorations up, and stick to it—so you're not fussing with tinsel and lights all month long. And remember: the just-right amount of festive for your home is whatever makes you happy, no matter what your neighbors are doing.

○ **ENJOY:** Start new traditions. Ban the "should," and follow your heart. If that means escaping for some sunshine and eating pizza instead of wrapping presents and baking cookies . . . go for it! Everything that has to get done will get done—it always does!

# 20

## cleaning

Keeping your home tidy positively affects the way you feel.

Clean floors, cabinets, beds, windows, and air are all healthier and more comfortable to live in, of course, but they also all function better (leaving you more time to kick back and relax).

Don't let the idea of cleaning overwhelm you. Staying ahead of the mess doesn't mean permanently having a broom in one hand and a feather duster in the other. It doesn't even mean regularly giving up huge chunks of time. The key is simply knowing the best tools and methods to tackle the job—and conquering a little bit of clutter daily, instead of your whole home in one go.

Maximize your cleaning efficiency with our helpful hit list of tricks and shortcuts for the most common mess-producing culprits in your house—from shedding pets to dusty blinds. And while you're at it, get your cleaning kit up to par with our all-star lineup of trusty helpmates. Attention: you're now entering a happy, dirt-free zone.

AUSTIN
Sara Oswalt
Fashion/Interior Stylist

# the basics

**1. Vacuum Cleaner** Canister versus upright comes down to ease of use and personal choice. Strong suction and attachment selection are key—and, if you have allergies, a HEPA filter is recommended.

**2. Rubber Dish Gloves** Slip-resistant fingertips ensure a firm hold; foam or cotton lining absorbs sweat, so dish-duty is a bit cooler.

**3. Surface Scrubber** Look for a comfortable grip, extra-stiff bristles, and an angled tip. Also, check that the label says "non-scratch."

**4. Carpet Beater** This is the best tool for getting ground-in dirt out of rugs with a deep pile. Note: a proper outdoor space for rug beating is a must.

**5. Dustpan** Look for one with a deep pan and rubber edge.

**6. Broom and Hand Brush** Natural bristles are the way to go, but don't get them wet. If that's a concern, stick with synthetic bristles (either polypropylene or PVC).

**7. Windex** This is so much more than a glass cleaner; use it on porcelain sinks, enamel stoves—even chrome appliances.

**8. Spray Bottle** Mix your own "green" cleaners; write the recipe directly on the bottle. (Hint: Apartment Therapy has tons of recipes on the site!)

**9. Feather Duster** Ostrich feathers trap dirt best. Black feathers are more effective than lighter ones (because they're softer).

**10. Murphy Oil Soap** The best option for treated hardwood floors and furniture, leather, vinyl, and ceramic surfaces. *Note:* Avoid use on unfinished wood.

**11. White Vinegar** This all-natural wonder removes mineral deposits, mold, and spots from drinking glasses; it even cleans your drains.

**12. Bon Ami** An environmentally friendly all-purpose scrubbing powder that has been around for almost 130 years. Sometimes we think it has superpowers.

**13. Cleaning Supply Caddy** Turn your most-used essentials mobile. Bonus: the caddy helps you keep track of what you're running out of.

**14. Sponge** Color-code your sponge system: one for the tub, another for the counters, and so forth.

**15. Magic Eraser** It cleans certain stains from most surfaces with the addition of a little water. Warning: test on a small area first to avoid permanent scratches.

**16. Mop and 2.5-gallon Bucket** Mops with removable heads make for easier cleanup. A bucket this size holds a mop but also doubles as a vessel for soaking clothes.

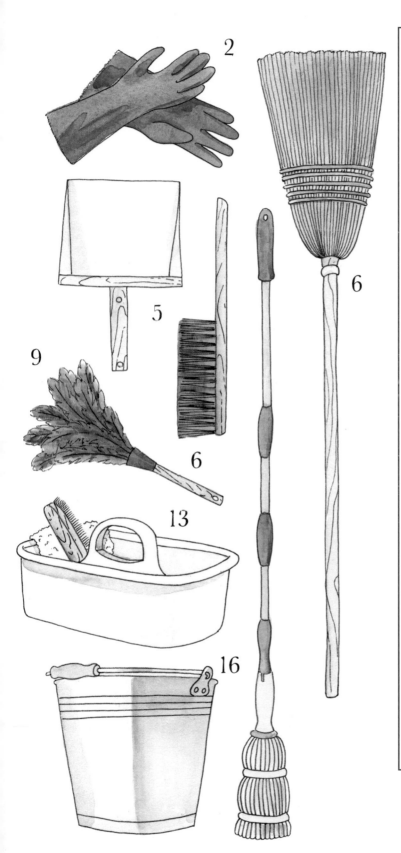

2

5

9

13

16

6

6

## cheat sheet: **good-bye, stains**

**RED WINE:** Mix one teaspoon (colorless) dish soap in a cup of hydrogen peroxide. If the stain is still wet, blot the area, apply the mixture, and then continue to blot and reapply as needed. If the stain is already dry, apply the mixture and let sit for half an hour as a presoak before laundering or dry-cleaning.

**INK:** Hair spray and hand sanitizer both work as a presoak before laundering. Generously cover the stain with whichever you have handy. Let it sit for ten minutes, and then wash normally.

**COFFEE:** Mix equal parts white vinegar and water in a spray bottle. Spritz the stain; then blot gently with a wet towel. If it doesn't fade, try mixing 1 tablespoon of ammonia with 1 cup of water. Dab the area with this mixture until the stain begins to disappear.

**CRAYONS:** Minor marks: Make a paste from two parts baking soda and one part warm water. Scrub the area using a damp rag. Major marks: Spray the area with WD-40. Wipe with a clean, dry rag.

**GREASE:** Cornmeal is a natural absorbent. Sprinkle directly onto the stain, let sit for at least twenty minutes, and then vacuum up the cornmeal or shake it off over a trash can. Dry-clean after.

# quick cleaning tips

## dust busters

**BLINDS, CEILING FANS, AND BASEBOARDS:** Wipe them down with a fabric softener sheet. It dusts and lightly polishes in one easy step.

**FRAGILE ITEMS** (artwork, lamp shades, lace curtains): Use a blow dryer—set to low and cool—to gently send dust flying. Just be prepared to wipe up the dust after it lands elsewhere.

## pet patrol

**PET HAIR:** Run a damp dishwashing glove over any surface, and hair will stick right to it. Rinse the dirty glove in the sink when you're through, and hang to dry.

**PET ODOR:** For indoor cats, look for clay-based litter; it clumps faster and absorbs odor. For dogs, brush and bathe them frequently (at least once every three weeks). And when accidents occur, spray Nature's Miracle Stain & Odor Remover directly on the area.

## sticky messes

**GET STICKERS OFF WINDOWS OR WALLS:** Slather a little mayonnaise over the sticker; it dissolves the adhesive after a few minutes. Wipe clean with a damp rag.

**REMOVE GUM OR CANDLE WAX FROM HARD SURFACES:** Rub with ice to help harden the wax or gum. Then scrape it off with an old credit card.

## mineral buildup

**SHOWERHEADS:** For metal heads, remove and boil for fifteen minutes in a solution of one part white vinegar to eight parts water. For plastic heads, remove and soak in a solution of equal parts white vinegar and water.

**KETTLES:** Fill the kettle with equal parts white vinegar and water. Bring to a boil; then let sit overnight. The bluish-green dots should wash right out the next morning.

## rug revival

**FLIP IT:** Twice a year, turn your rugs over and vacuum them from the reverse side. It's a simple way to get out ground-in dirt.

**REVIVE ANIMAL-SKIN RUGS:** Sprinkle cornmeal over the surface; let it sit for one hour. Then vacuum on low using the upholstery attachment.

## streak-free glass

**MIRRORS:** Spray with glass cleaner, and wipe with an industrial-size coffee filter or newspaper. Both options wipe the glass clean while absorbing the liquid. Bonus: they contain less lint, which means you get a streak-free surface with fewer swipes.

**EXTERIOR WINDOWS:** Twice a year, remove screens and thoroughly clean windows. First, sweep away built-up gunk, like cobwebs. Then spray with the hose. Lastly, spritz with glass cleaner and wipe clean (with newspaper to remove grease).

STREAK-FREE GLASS

RUG CARE

PET MESSES

DUST BUSTERS

## 21

# repairs

Your home shouldn't just be beautiful; it should be in good working order, too.

Maintaining that ideal state is a never-ending process involving work, patience, creativity, and, often, a good sense of humor.

The easiest way to take care of your home is to get to know it. As soon as you move in, locate the water main, listen to the sound the toilet makes when it flushes, take note of your average heating bill. The better you understand the ins and outs of your place—quirks and all—the faster you'll recognize when something is wrong and take action.

And since repairs are inevitable, it pays—or, we should say, saves—to know how to fix the little things. A leaky faucet or running toilet could cost hundreds if you hire a repairman. But in most cases, you can fix it yourself in twenty minutes. Brush up on your handyman skills (or learn some, if they're nonexistent) and get your tool kit up to speed with our quick and easy guide to the most common household problems—and the tools you need to fix them.

LOS ANGELES
Judy Kameon + Erik Otsea
Landscape Designer + Outdoor
Furniture Designer
son, Ian

# the basics

**1. Spackle** An interior/exterior vinyl filler that covers most holes and cracks in the wall. For wood surfaces, use epoxy filler instead.

**2. Laser Level** Turns leveling, marking, and hanging pictures or shelves into a one-person job.

**3. Multihead Screwdriver** The functionality of ten screwdrivers in one space-saving package.

**4. Voltage Tester** Safely and easily identifies "hot" wires before doing electrical work.

**5. Utility Knife** A retractable blade and safety lock are key.

**6. Assorted Hardware** Build a kit of nuts, bolts, washers, anchors, and nails in various sizes.

**7. Metal Tape Measure** It should be at least one inch wide, so it doesn't bend when extended.

**8. Painter's and Duct Tape** Duct tape for tougher, utilitarian jobs (repairing tarps or bicycle seats). Painter's tape for paint jobs (of course!), but also good for impromptu labeling of items around the house.

**9. WD-40** Handy for so many things: loosening rusty hinges, repelling roaches, getting gum out of hair . . .

**10. 18V (or higher) Cordless Drill and Bits** Splurge on a model with a lithium-ion battery; it's lighter and will last longer.

**11. Steel-head Hammer** A leather or rubber handle is more comfortable for longer use.

**12. Locking Pliers or Vise Grips** They work in lieu of a clamp and are great for loosening stubborn screws.

**13. Wrench** Look for one that includes a ratcheting feature; you won't have to remove and refit the wrench after every single turn.

**14. Needle-nose Pliers** Opt for a pair with a built-in wire cutter to save time.

**15. Putty Knife** A coated steel head makes for easy cleanup.

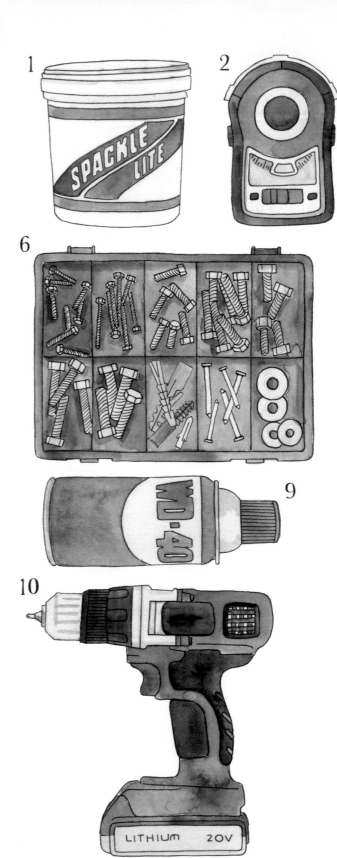

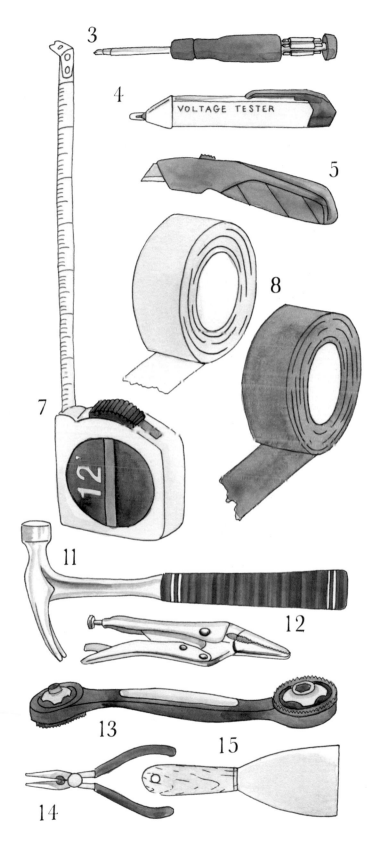

# fix it yourself

## quiet squeaky door hinges

Spray WD-40 directly onto the hinges, slowly swinging the door back and forth to work the liquid into the grooves. The squeaking should stop instantly. If that doesn't work, try lifting the door pins 2 to 3 inches out of the hinges. Rub a little 3-In-One oil directly onto the pin with a damp rag. Let dry (about five minutes); then slide the pins back into place.

## hide minor(ish) scratches on stained wood surfaces

For shallow scratches, mix equal parts olive oil and lemon juice in a cup. Pour onto a microfiber cloth, and rub in the direction of the scratch until the mark disappears. If the scratch goes deeper than the finish, naturally dye the scratched area with used, still-damp coffee grounds—place a thin layer over the scratch, let it sit for fifteen minutes, and wipe clean. Then rub the skin of a raw almond, walnut, or Brazil nut (pick the closest color match to your wood stain) along the mark. This should fill and mask the scratch.

## silence creaking wood floors

As a temporary solution, sprinkle talcum powder over the noisy bit of flooring. Using a paintbrush, work the powder into the cracks. Wipe up any leftover powder from the surface area—and enjoy the silence.

# fix it yourself (continued)

### fill a crack in your drywall

Using Spackle and a putty knife, fill the crack completely. Don't worry about getting this area flush with the rest of the wall just yet. Blast the spot with a hair dryer set to low for fifteen minutes. Once dry, sand with a piece of fine-grit sandpaper until smooth and level. Cover the area with primer, and then paint.

### stop a dripping faucet

A dirty aerator (the little mesh piece in the faucet head) is usually to blame. The fix is simple: First, block the drain with a kitchen towel, so you don't lose any parts. Unscrew the tip of the faucet with your fingers. If it's too tight, use a wrench to carefully loosen it. Remove all the components, taking note of the order in which they belong. Wash each piece with warm, soapy water, and reassemble the parts in order. No more drips!

### speed up a slow-moving drain

Dealing with daily clogs? Pour one cup of baking soda, then one cup of vinegar, down your drain. Let it work its magic for two to three hours; then turn the warm water on for two minutes to flush the pipes. Repeat if necessary. This works for hair in the bathtub as well as food in the kitchen sink.

### hide cat-scratched upholstery

First of all, don't get too grumpy with your furry friend. Look at the rips as an opportunity to personalize your furniture. Sew a collection of vintage patches (or even contrasting fabric) over the tattered upholstery. If you need to, sew a couple of small patches together in order to cover more surface area—layering only ups the cool factor.

### level a rocking toilet

Before doing anything drastic, try tightening the bolts around the base. If it's still shaky, grab some plastic shims from your local hardware store and slip them into the gap between the bottom of your toilet and the floor.

### fix a cupboard door that won't stay shut

There's no need to replace a cabinet door that keeps swinging open. In the short term, buy some heavy-duty magnets; attach one side to the inside of the door, the other side to the cabinet. And, as easy as that, your cupboard will stay securely shut for the foreseeable future.

### get a sliding door back on track

If your sliding door is constantly coming off its track, it's probably because the track is either bent or flattened from wear. Reshape it, and it'll be good as new. Find a piece of lumber that's just thick enough to fit into the center slot of your tracks. (You want minimal space between the wood and the track.) Make sure the wood is secure; then use a mallet to pound the outside of the track guides back into shape.

SQUEAKY DOOR

LEAKY FAUCET

PATCHED FURNITURE

LEVEL TOILET

# 5 easy design updates you've (probably) never thought of . . .

1 Love the look of tile but can't afford it? Stencil your favorite pattern on finished plywood to use as flooring.

2 Forget expensive slipcovers. Have one made from a vintage wool blanket to save on fabric costs.

3 Replicate the look of traditional wall molding with painter's tape! Simply tape the desired pattern on your wall, paint (a dark color works best), and remove the tape.

4 Get the lo-fi, cozy look of mismatched sofa cushions (or hide worn spots) with a colorful pillowcase. Just slip one over the cushion, and pin excess fabric if necessary. It's cheaper than upholstery—and so much easier.

5 Have specific over-the-desk storage needs but can't fork over the cash for something custom? Prop an antique metal bed frame against the wall, and add shelves, file holders, and clips as needed.

> "A place for everything and everything in its place."

# 22

# getting organized

You've most likely heard this old adage—and it's still solid advice today. But, if you ask us, the biggest secret to feeling good in your home is a modern addition to that idea: "Leave a little space for things you don't have."

Breathing room is essential to creating a sense of calm and comfort. It's only achieved when not every surface, closet, cabinet, and shelf is totally full. A good rule of thumb is to leave at least 10 percent of a room "unfilled."

To get there, you must first streamline what you own. Less clutter and fewer choices automatically lead to increased peace of mind. Then, you have to stay organized. In the long run, it's a huge time-saver—meaning, you can spend more of your day doing the things you love.

You'll find tons of tips and tools (divided by room) in this chapter to help you on your quest for order. And you can stay inspired by this idea: Don't get organized because you're "supposed" to. Get organized as a way to facilitate your own happiness.

CHICAGO
Lisa + Joel Santos
Gourmet Grocer/Chef +
Computer Developer

# the basics

## kitchen

**1. Countertop Utensil Jar** Free up drawer space by storing larger utensils out in the open.

**2. Plastic-bag Holder** Stuff bags into a designated container for grab-and-go convenience.

**3. Pot-lid Organizer** "File" lids (instead of stacking them) to save cabinet space.

**4. Expandable Drawer Organizer** Organize every inch of every drawer: cutlery in the kitchen, beauty supplies in the bathroom, socks and undies in the bedroom.

**5. Chalkboard Stickers** Label leftovers with the day they were cooked or dry goods that have been transferred to airtight containers.

## tv room

**6. Cord-control Box** Hide tangled cords and whole power strips in every room.

**7. Sonos Wireless Speakers** Music where you want it. Control this system from your smartphone or desktop.

**8. External Hard Drive** Truth: the more you store digitally, the less clutter you have. Schedule an automatic backup to an external hard drive every two weeks.

**9. DVD/CD Binder** Can't part with your old DVDs or CDs? Toss the cases, and store them in space-saving binders.

**10. Remote-control Box** Keep your main remote handy, but collect all those other clickers in a decorative box.

## bathroom

**11. Hair-tool Organizer** Look for one with integrated outlets for extra convenience and cord control.

**12. Under-the-Counter Shelving** Use them under the sink or in the kitchen, garage, or any closet to double your vertical space for storage.

**13. Hooks** Get pretty ones for hanging things in plain sight, and more utilitarian styles for neatly stashing stuff inside a cabinet.

**14. First-Aid Kit** Store emergency essentials in one grab-and-go container. Visit the redcross.org for a list of recommended supplies.

**15. Magnetic Strip** Install one in your medicine cabinet to corral bobby pins, tweezers, and other metal sundries.

CHALKBOARD

STICKERS

FIRST AID KIT

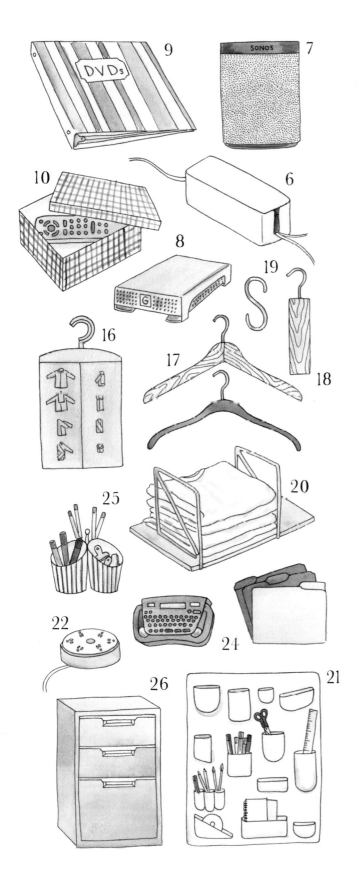

## closet

**16. Folding Board** It guarantees tight, uniform folds, meaning you can squeeze more into your drawers.

**17. Skinny Non-slip Hangers and Wooden Coat Hangers** Save valuable inches with this combination: hang everything but coats and blazers—which lose their shape if not on proper coat hangers—from slim, non-slip hangers.

**18. Cedar Hanging Block** Cedar repels moths—and keeps closets smelling fresh. Tip: lightly sand to renew the scent.

**19. S-Hook** Loop one over your closet rail and hang everything from bags to scarves to oversize necklaces.

**20. Closet Shelf Divider** Turn a long shelf into many useful sections for neatly stacking pants, sweaters, or tees.

## office

**21. Wall Organizer** Look for one with dedicated compartments for storing desktop essentials.

**22. Power Station** Because one outlet is never enough! Keep a small station on your desk for charging gadgets.

**23. Cord Organizer** Look for one that safely sticks to the back of furniture and allows cords to easily pop in and out.

**24. Color-coded Files and Label Maker** Designate colors for different types of documents; it will make them easier to find months (or years) later.

**25. Desk Caddy** Pick something small to house items that usually wind up homeless on your desktop.

**26. Filing Cabinet** Stackable cabinets give you the option of adding on, should you need to, down the road.

## entryway

**27. Wall-hung Storage** Hanging hooks. Hideaway cubbies. Mounted drawers. Build the system that works for you (and your drop zone).

**28. Large Durable Basket** Create an out-box for things you need to remember to take with you: dry cleaning, gym bag, etc.

**29. Shoe Bench** Save space with a bench that doubles as shoe storage. Just don't let it become a permanent home.

**30. Mail Sorter** Do yourself a favor and sort mail as it comes into the house. It takes seconds!

**31. Umbrella Stand** Essential on rainy days but also a handy, temporary landing spot for some after-school sports equipment (bats or tennis racquets).

# the room-by-room guide to an
# **organized home**

## in the kitchen

**LET FUNCTION DICTATE STORAGE.**
Keep coffee near the coffeemaker, knives by your cutting boards, and towels next to the sink. Similarly, stow your cooking supplies, including spices, within arm's reach of the stove.

**IF DRAWER SPACE IS AT A PREMIUM,** think about storing flatware in pretty containers on your countertop. Grab-and-go silverware speeds things up come mealtime and leaves drawers free for bigger items.

**WHEN POSSIBLE, BUY SETS OF DINNERWARE, GLASSES, AND STORAGE CONTAINERS** instead of mixing and matching. Everything stacks neatly away, making the best use of your shelf space.

**TAPE YOUR MOST-USED RECIPES TO THE INSIDE OF A CABINET DOOR** for instant access anytime. It saves precious countertop space when you're prepping meals and keeps you from ever having to pull out a cookbook or go online.

**TRANSFER DRY GOODS** like grains, sugar, and cereal to matching airtight containers, which creates visual cohesiveness in chaotic pantries, while keeping everything fresher longer.

## in the entryway

**THINK OF THIS SPACE AS A TEMPORARY LANDING SPOT,** not a permanent drop zone. Pick one day per week to sort through the coats, accessories, and shoes stashed there. Relocate anything that's not being used to its real home.

**KEEP YOURSELF FROM SPINNING IN CIRCLES** by setting up the entryway to mimic the way you shed your gear. If you drop your keys first and take off your shoes last, for instance, place the key-ring holder closest to the door and the shoe cubbies farthest away.

**HAVE A PLAN FOR THE LITTLE STUFF.** Hats, gloves, earmuffs—it only takes minutes for these things to pile up. If you have the space, give each family member a cubby for housing these items. If that's not an option, dedicate one basket to everyone's accessories. But keep a watchful eye on what's getting tossed in there (and how long it stays).

**STORE A SMALL KIT OF "MINOR EMERGENCY" ESSENTIALS BY THE DOOR:** a compact umbrella, a spare phone charger/portable battery, an extra pair of glasses, spare keys, some cash, and a public-transit card or two. You'll thank yourself later, when you're dashing out the door.

**SORT LOOSE POCKET CHANGE** (quarters, nickels, dimes, pennies) instead of tossing it all into one overflowing bowl. Get into the habit of doing this as soon as you walk in the door. You'll be surprised how quickly those coins add up to serious cash.

## in the bathroom

**SPEED UP YOUR MORNING DASH.**
Keep grooming essentials (moisturizer, daily cosmetics, go-to hair products) out and easily accessible. Organize everything on a small tray to contain the chaos and stop products from taking over your countertop.

**SAVE SPACE (AND MONEY) BY BUYING SHAMPOO, CONDITIONER, AND LIQUID SOAP IN BULK SIZES,** then transferring them to smaller, refillable containers for the shower. Store the larger bottles.

**NOT ALL BATHROOMS ARE CREATED EQUAL.** Be realistic about the storage space in yours (overcrowding will just up your frustration). Make sure the most essential items have a home; then add things as needed.

**DON'T STASH THE TP!** Keep the extra toilet paper rolls out in a decorative basket or bin, so you (and your guests) never find yourself awkwardly "stranded." No one wants to rifle through cabinets at that particular moment.

**GO VERTICAL.** This is time-tested organization advice in general, but especially in the bathroom. Look for opportunities to mount above-the-toilet shelves. Or try turning a multilevel fruit basket into extra storage by hanging it from the ceiling.

GRAB-AND-GO
SILVERWARE

REFILLABLE
CONTAINERS

AIRTIGHT JARS

TEMPORARY
LANDING SPOT

BLANKET STORAGE

BASKET
NETWORK

INSPIRATION
BOARD

# in the office

**ONLY KEEP THINGS ON THE DESK THAT YOU USE DAILY**—no exceptions. Everything else should have a proper, out-of-sight home. (Except maybe a plant—we'll allow it.)

**DON'T NEGLECT DIGITAL ORGANIZATION.** Clean off your (virtual) desktop daily—and back up once every two weeks. With so much of your life online, even a perfect-looking physical space won't be much help if your computer is a disaster.

**DISCONNECT FROM THE CHAOS.** Invest in a wireless mouse, keyboard, and printer—and forever free yourself from that tangled pile of cords surrounding your monitor.

**SET UP A PHYSICAL IN-BOX,** but schedule fifteen minutes per day to deal with the things that land there. File or digitize anything important. Shred or recycle everything else.

**A LITTLE INSPIRATION GOES A LONG WAY.** Hanging artwork or creating a bulletin board of things you love will keep you motivated while you're in the work zone. Make sure it's minimal, though. Otherwise, you run the risk of inspiration turning into distraction.

# in the tv room

**SET UP YOUR MEDIA CENTER AWAY FROM "THE ELEMENTS."** Excessive sunlight, smoke, and water from pipes, radiators, or air conditioners can shorten the life span of electronics, records, CDs, and DVDs.

**KEEP FAMILY PHOTOS EASILY ACCESSIBLE** via an external hard drive (or in your cloud). If you're missing the photo album experience, have a select few "best of" collections printed via sites like Blurb or Shutterfly.

**LIMIT THE NUMBER OF CONSOLES**—and remotes—in your life by opting for all-in-one gadgetry, like a gaming console that doubles as a Blu-ray player and connects to Netflix.

**THINK ABOUT UPDATING MEDIA-CABINET DOORS WITH METAL MESH PANELS.** Your remote control's gamma rays can zip right through the holes, so you can hide your cable box and other gadgets inside and still change the channel.

**THIS IS A PLACE TO GET COZY, BUT DON'T LET EXTRA THROW BLANKETS TAKE OVER.** Consider stowing them in a trunk or folding them on top of a vintage luggage rack.

# in the bedroom closet

**SEPARATE YOUR CLOTHES ON THE CLOSET RAIL** by type (shirts, skirts, dresses, and so forth), then color—lightest to darkest. It's how your eye naturally takes things in and will speed up those morning "what the heck am I going to wear today?" moments.

**MAKE THE MOST OF YOUR SHOE STORAGE** (whether it's on the floor or a shoe rack) by stowing each pair heel to toe, so they nestle more tightly together. Or, if you have the depth, line them up one shoe in front of the other instead of side by side. That way you can squeeze twice as many pairs on one shelf.

**OBEY THE FOLD, HANG, FILE RULE:**
- *fold:* Jeans, sweatshirts, sweaters, socks, and anything bulky
- *hang:* Dresses, skirts, blazers, coats, suits, and almost everything you dry clean
- *file* (i.e., fold and store vertically): T-shirts, underwear, shorts, and pajamas

**KEEP TRACK OF WHAT YOU'RE STORING ON THOSE TIP-TOP SHELVES.** Fasten a mirror to the bottom of the shelf above, or directly to the wall behind, an out-of-reach shelf. You can see every last handbag you've stashed away without having to leave the floor.

**BUILD A BASKET NETWORK:** two for laundry (one dark, one light), one for dry cleaning, and another for clothes that need repair. It'll keep the temptation to toss things on the floor (or over a chair) at bay.

# meet the homeowners. . .

**John Berg + Jennifer Desmond**
EAST HAMPTON, NEW YORK
Architect + Wine Consultant
*bergdesignarchitecture.com*
*jenniferdesmond.com*

**Brenda + David Bergen**
**+ son, Daniel**
CHICAGO
Creative Director/Designer, Wink Design +
Digital Media Consultant
*wink-design.com*

**Allison + Ryan Burke**
AUSTIN
Founder, Allison Burke Interior Design +
Partner, A Parallel Architecture
*allison-burke.com*
*aparallel.com*

**Mary + Lou Castelli**
**+ daughter, Sienna + sons Colton,**
**Rex, Bo**
MAPLEWOOD, NEW JERSEY
Mother + Private Equity Professional
*ljlcapital.com*

**Christopher Coleman + Angel**
**Sanchez**
ELIZAVILLE, NEW YORK
Interior Designer + Fashion Designer
*ccinteriordesign.com*
*christophercolemancollection.com*
*angelsanchezusa.com*

**Tim Cuppett + Marco Rini**
AUSTIN
Founder, Tim Cuppett Architects + Founder,
David Wilson Garden Design
*cuppettarchitects.com*
*dwgd.com*

**Jessica + Scott Davis**
**+ son, Bryan + daughter, Lucy**
MILLBURN, NEW JERSEY
Designer, Nest Studio +
Marketing, Nickelodeon
*nest-studio-home.com*

**Laura Jay Freedman**
LOS ANGELES
Shop Owner, Broken English Jewelry
*brokenenglishjewelry.com*

**Arthur Garcia-Clemente +**
**Kristin Over**
CHICAGO
Workplace Designer +
Freelance Interior Designer

**Paige + Smoot Hull**
**+ son, Pierce + daughters Eisley,**
**Cameron**
ROUND TOP, TEXAS
Co-owners, The Vintage Round Top
*thevintageroundtop.com*

**Emily Johnston**
NEW YORK CITY
Photographer
*emily-johnston.com*

**Judy Kameon + Erik Otsea**
**+ son, Ian**
LOS ANGELES
Landscape Designer/Outdoor Furniture
Designer + Photographer/Outdoor
Furniture Designer
*elysianlandscapes.com*
*plainair.com*

**Michelle + Dave Kohanzo**
**+ daughter, Emily**
**+ sons Connor, Henry, Everett**
BARRINGTON, ILLINOIS
CEO, Land of Nod + Banker, Northern Trust
*landofnod.com*

**Christiane Lemieux + Joshua Young**
**+ daughter, Isabelle + son, William**
EAST HAMPTON, NEW YORK
Founder, Dwell Studio/Executive Creative
Director, Wayfair + Real Estate Developer,
The Related Companies
*dwellstudio.com*
*wayfair.com*
*related.com*

**Susan + Kevin Lennon**
**+ daughter, Griffin**
VENICE BEACH
Owner, SHOP by h. bleu + Founder,
Lennon Design
*shophbleu.com*

**Deborah Nevins**
EAST COAST
Landscape Designer, Deborah Nevins &
Associates Inc.
*dnalandscape.com*

**Eric Oliver + Thea Goodman**
**+ daughter, Esme + son, Ethan**
CHICAGO
Professor, University of Chicago + Author

**Sara Oswalt**
AUSTIN
Fashion/Interior Stylist, Purveyor Design
*saraoswalt.com*
*purveyordesign.com*

**Lulu Powers + Stephen Danelian**
LOS ANGELES
The Entertainologist + Founder, MeeLocal
*lulupowers.com*
*meelocal.com*

**Dean + Michael Renaud**
CHICAGO
Principal, South Social & Home + Creative
Director, Pitchfork
*southsocialandhome.com*

**Moon Rhee + Heyja Do**
BROOKLYN
Shop Owners, Dear: Rivington+
*dearrivington.com*

**Maxwell Ryan + daughter, Ursula**
NEW YORK CITY
CEO & Founder, Apartment Therapy
*apartmenttherapy.com*

**Lisa + Joel Santos**
CHICAGO
Owner/Chef, Southport Grocery and Café +
Credit Risk Computer Developer
*southportgrocery.com*

**Ruthie Sommers + Luke McDonough**
**+ daughters Eloise, Bailey, Posey**
LOS ANGELES
Mother, Friend, Interior Designer +
CEO, AirMedia
*ruthiesommers.wordpress.com*
*ruthiesommers.com*
*airmedia.com*

**Taylor Swaim**
BROOKLYN
J.Crew Brand Creative

**Michele Varian + Brad Roberts**
NEW YORK CITY
Product Designer & Store Owner, Michele
Varian Shop + Musician, Crash Test Dummies
*michelevarian.com*
*crashtestdummies.com*

**Erin Williamson + Ben Roy**
**+ sons Ike, Luke**
AUSTIN
Blogger & Interior Designer, Design Crisis +
Software Engineering Manager, HP
*design-crisis.com*

**Anne Ziegler + Scott Mason**
LOS ANGELES
Trend Forecaster + Entertainment Executive
*anneziegler.com*

# resources

## copyright

**Paige + Smoot Hull—Pages 4–5**
**Daybed Slipcover:** made by homeowners from Navy surplus canvas, theseedboxantiques.blogspot.com
**Grain Sack Throw Pillows (on daybed):** made by homeowners, thevintageroundtop.com
**Wall Sconces (above daybed):** made by homeowners, cow feed sifters with burlap liner
**Curtains:** IKEA, ikea.com
**Curtain Rods:** made by homeowners, repurposed plumbing supplies
**Wood Ceiling Panels:** made by homeowners, salvaged siding from Habitat for Humanity ReStore, habitat.org/restores
**Trunk (used as coffee table):** vintage from a garage sale
**Wooden Window Screens (on fireplace):** vintage from a garage sale
**French Green Glass Bottle Vases:** vintage, thevintageroundtop.com
**Sofa:** gift. Target slipcover, target.com
**Feed Sack Throw Pillows (on sofa):** made by homeowners, thevintageroundtop.com
**Arrow Light Fixture (above sofa):** Round Top Antiques Fair, roundtoptexasantiques.com
**Bar Stools (at kitchen counter):** vintage, roundtoptexasantiques.com

## PART ONE
## setting up your home

**Eric Oliver + Thea Goodman—Pages 10–11**
**Retro Chevron Table Lamp:** Jonathan Adler, jonathanadler.com
**Sofa:** Jonathan Adler, jonathanadler.com
**Purple Velvet Chairs:** gift
**Marble Side Table:** Saarinen Side Table, dwr.com
**Ottomans:** X Bench, jonathanadler.com
**Dotted Silk Throw Pillows:** John Robshaw, johnrobshaw.com
**Mirrored Side Table:** Horchow, horchow.com
**Glass-Top Side Tables:** Jonathan Adler, jonathanadler.com
**Abstract Painting:** by Keiko Nemeth, keikonemeth.com
**Rug:** Pat Nixon Rug, jonathanadler.com

## getting the right flow

**Erin Williamson + Ben Roy—Page 18**
**Tan Elite Leather Sofa:** eBay.com
**Black Leather Chesterfield Sofa:** vintage Ethan Allen, craigslist.com
**Lucite Coffee Table:** craigslist.com
**Malayer Area Rug:** eBay.com
**Black and White Throw Pillows:** West Elm Outlet

**Gray & White Throw Pillows:** Stone Textile Studio, stonetextilestudio.com
**Maitland-Smith Side Table:** vintage
**Glass Table Lamp:** eBay.com
**Curtains:** HPD, halfpricedrapes.com

## style

**Christiane Lemieux + Joshua Young—Page 24**
**Chevron Area Rug:** Madeline Weinrib, madelineweinrib.com
**Sofa in Magnus Mineral Fabric:** Dwell Studio, dwellstudio.com
**Coffee Table:** vintage
**Hans Leather Chair and Ottoman:** Dwell Studio, dwellstudio.com
**Floor Lamp:** vintage
**Curtains:** The Shade Store, theshadestore.com
**Wall Sconce:** vintage, eBay.com
**Curtis French Oak Side Table:** Dwell Studio, dwellstudio.com
**Urchin Shiny Gold Objet (above mantel):** Dwell Studio, dwellstudio.com
**Monet Gold Votive (on side table):** Dwell Studio, dwellstudio.com

## color

**Mary + Lou Castelli—Page 30**
**Cabinetry:** IKEA, ikea.com
**Powder-Coated Cabinet Hardware:** hardware, Simon's Hardware and Bath, simonsny.com. Powder-coating fabricated by Empire Metal Finishing, empiremetal.net
**Countertops:** Corian, dupont.com

## walls

**Michele Varian + Brad Roberts—Page 36**
**Plume Wallpaper:** by Michele Varian, michelevarian.com

## floors

**Anne Ziegler + Scott Mason—Page 40**
**Kitchen Range:** American Range, americanrange.com
**Hand Towels:** Creative Women, nickeykehoe.com
**Pots and Pans:** Sur la Table, surlatable.com

## windows

**Jessica + Scott Davis—Page 46**
**Curtains:** Target, target.com
**Curtain Rods:** Pottery Barn, potterybarn.com
**Wall-Mounted Light Fixture:** Restoration Hardware, restorationhardware.com

**Framed Art Panel:** by Robert Crowder & Company, robertcrowder.com
**Bedside Table:** South Seas Side Cart, serenaandlily.com
**Quilt:** Target, target.com

## lighting

**Maxwell Ryan—Page 52**
**Dining Room Chairs:** Hay, hay.dk
**Gray Lambswool Skins:** Gray Gotland Sheepskin, huset.com
**Wall Mirror:** Bobo Intriguing Objects, bobointriguingobjects.com
**Dining Room Table:** built by homeowner
**Pendant Lights:** Bobo Intriguing Objects, bobointriguingobjects.com

## art

**Dean + Michael Renaud—Page 56**
**Framed Photography:** by David Sampson, davidcsampson.com
**Rug:** estate sale in Los Angeles

## PART TWO
## living in your home

**Mary + Lou Castelli—Pages 70–71**
**Wall Paint:** Benjamin Moore "Barely Teal," benjaminmoore.com
**Dining Table:** family heirloom
**Dining Chairs:** family heirlooms (updated with paint)
**Delta IV Pendant Light:** Rich Brilliant Willing, richbrilliantwilling.com
**Custom Curtains:** West Elm, westelm.com. Stripes are Designers Guild fabric, designersguild.com
**Holy Stool:** by Francois Chambard, umproject.com

## entryways

**Opener**
**Deborah Nevins—Pages 72–73**
**Vintage Folding Chairs:** gift

**The Southwest-Gone-Bright Entry**
**Sara Oswalt—Pages 74–75**
**Bubble Chandelier:** by Jean Pelle, pelledesigns.com
**Door Paint:** Behr "Beluga," behr.com
**Mismatched Wall Hooks:** Anthropologie, anthropologie.com
**Framed Posters:** Public School Creative Collaborative, gotopublicschool.com
**Red Frames:** Art on Fifth, arton5th.com
**Wood Bench:** vintage from Sacramento, CA
**Southwestern Rug:** gift

### The "Quick" Entry
**Moon Rhee + Heyja Do—Pages 76–77**
**Wall-Mounted Hat Rack:** vintage
**Wooden Bench:** vintage
**1970's Bicycle:** vintage
**Red Pom-Pom Dusters:** vintage

### The Indoor/Outdoor Mudroom
**Anne Ziegler + Scott Mason—Pages 78–79**
**Antique French Chair:** Penine Hart Antiques and Art, peninehart.com
**Vintage French Table:** One Kings Lane, onekingslane.com
**Large White Ceramic Bowl:** vintage
**Framed Camera Print:** by Hugo Guinness, johnderian.com
**Woven Doormat:** Haus Interior, hausinterior.com
**Dip-Dyed Stool:** Serena & Lily, serenaandlily.com

### The Never-Too-Thin Entry
**Maxwell Ryan—Pages 80–81**
**Half-Circle Side Table:** Bobo Intriguing Objects, bobointriguingobjects.com
**Printed Runners:** by Madeline Weinrib, madelineweinrib.com
**Table Lamp:** vintage
**Wall-Mounted Coat Rack:** Eames Hang-It-All, dwr.com

### The Compact Cottage Mudroom
**Tim Cuppett + Marco Rini—Pages 82–83**
**Paint Color:** Benjamin Moore "Statton Blue," benjaminmoore.com
**Wall-Mounted Hooks:** made by homeowners
**Doorstop:** Scully & Scully, scullyandscully.com

## living spaces
### Opener
**Judy Kameon + Erik Otsea—Pages 84–85**
**Vintage Kilim Rug:** Long Beach Antique Market, longbeachantiquemarket.com
**Sofa:** Futurama, futuramafurniturela.com
**Tile Coffee Table:** Plain Air, plainair.com
**Velvet Armchair:** Cadillac Jacks furniture
**Vintage Rocking Chair:** gift
**Artwork:** by Judy Kameon
**Side Tables:** made by homeowners
**Vintage Green Lamp:** Retro Gallery, retroglass.com
**David Cressey Lamp:** flea market
**Leather Moroccan Poofs:** Mosaik, e-mosaik.com
**Blue Throw:** Calypso, calypsostbarth.com/home

### The Out-of-Africa Living Room
**Sara Oswalt—Pages 86–89**
**Tufted Petrie Sofa:** Crate & Barrel, crateandbarrel.com
**Yellow Throw Pillows:** custom by Kelly Wearstler, kellywearstler.com

**Tall Table Lamp:** vintage from Sacramento, CA
**Side Tables:** vintage from San Antonio, TX
**Leather and Chrome Chairs:** vintage from Round Top Antiques Fair, roundtoptexasantiques.com
**Wood Table (under window):** eBay.com
**Metal Table Light:** vintage from Round Top Antique Show, roundtoptexasantiques.com
**Leather Armchair and Footstool:** vintage from Sacramento, CA
**Robin Egg Blue Platter (on coffee table):** by Luna Garcia, lunagarcia.com
**Felt Coasters (on coffee table):** Feliz, felizsale.com
**Resin Durian Fruit Sculpture:** Gold Leaf Design Group, amazon.com
**Tie-Dye and Chrome Footstool:** base from Round Top Antiques Fair, roundtoptexasantiques.com. Fabric from Hickory Chair, hickorychair.com

### The Modern Green Den
**Mary + Lou Castelli—Pages 90–91**
**Area Rug:** TSAR Carpet, tsarusa.com
**Leather Jacobsen-Style Egg Chair:** In Mod, inmod.com
**Lacquer Coffee Table:** Jonathan Adler, jonathanadler.com
**Ruché Sofa:** Ligne Roset, ligne-roset-usa.com
**Stackable Powder-Coated Steel Trays (on coffee table):** Kaleido Trays, aplusrstore.com
**Black and Gold Bud Vases (on mantel):** CB2, cb2.com
**Black Resin Pig (on mantel):** by Harry Allen, aplusrstore.com
**Felt Pom-Pom Garland (on mantel):** Etsy.com
**Flute Side Tables:** by Roberto Barbieri, poliformusa.com
**Printed Curtains:** IKEA, ikea.com

### The Dipped-in-Gray Living Room
**Emily Johnston—Pages 92–93**
**Wall Paint:** Benjamin Moore "Gray Horse," benjaminmoore.com
**French Door Paint:** Benjamin Moore "Black," benjaminmoore.com
**Sofa:** vintage
**Gray Velvet Chairs:** vintage
**Large White Area Rug:** West Elm, westelm.com
**Pale Blue Rug:** Canvas Home, canvashomestore.com
**Lumbar Throw Pillows:** West Elm, westelm.com
**Black Stitch Throw Pillow:** Loopy Mango, loopymango.com
**Coffee Table:** Canvas Home, canvashomestore.com
**Side Table:** vintage
**Table Lamp:** CB2, cb2.com
**Reclaimed Wood Bookshelf:** Roost Home Furnishings, roostco.com
**Pendant Light:** IKEA, ikea.com
**Throw Blanket (on chair):** Hand & Cloth, handandcloth.org
**Wood Stump Side Table:** Z Gallerie, zgallerie.com
**Trio of Brown Vases (on bookshelf):** Heath Ceramics, heathceramics.com

**Framed Print (above sofa):** by Michael Hunter, michael-hunter.net

### The Moroccan Game Den
**Lulu Powers + Stephen Danelian—Pages 94–97**
**Wall Paint:** Benjamin Moore "Bainbridge Blue," benjaminmoore.com
**Yellow Sofa:** Rag Finders in LA
**Area Rug:** bought in Armenia
**Moroccan Leather Poufs:** Target, target.com
**Extra-Long Coffee Table:** vintage
**Framed Photograph (over sofa):** by Stephen Danelian
**Large Wall Mirror:** Brenda Antin in LA
**Low-Sitting Slipper Chairs:** Antique, darrenransdell.com
**Game Table:** gift
**Bar Cabinet:** Dovecote, dovecote-westport.com

### The Soft Traditional Living Room
**Maxwell Ryan—Pages 98–101**
**Elephant Stool Side Tables:** Bobo Intriguing Objects, bobointriguingobjects.com
**White Sofa:** March Sofa by Hickory Chair, hickorychair.com
**White Chair:** Laura Chair by Hickory Chair, hickorychair.com
**Gray Velvet Sofa:** March Sofa by Hickory Chair, hickorychair.com
**Modern Floor Lamp:** AJ Floor Lamp, dwr.com
**Curtains:** Basketweave Linen Curtains, restorationhardware.com
**Curtain Hardware:** Weathered Oak Hardware, restorationhardware.com
**Dippy Red Rugs:** The Rug Company, therugcompany.com
**Coffee Table:** vintage
**Shearling Rugs:** 3-Corner Field Farm, dairysheepfarm.com
**Wooden 3-Legged Stool:** vintage, bobointriguingobjects.com
**Squiggle Prints:** by Maxwell Ryan
**Collage Artwork:** by Emily Payne, emilypayne.net
**Painting of House:** by Mary Ryan
**Framed Cuban Dancing Photo:** by Tria Giovan, clicgallery.com
**Faux Fur Throw:** Restoration Hardware, restorationhardware.com
**Patterned Throw Pillows:** Judy Ross, judyrosstextiles.com

### The Dramatically Different Country Den
**Tim Cuppett + Marco Rini—Pages 102–03**
**Wall Paint:** Benjamin Moore "Black Knight," benjaminmoore.com
**Area Rug:** vintage from James Powell Antiques in Austin
**Wall-Mounted Portrait Lights:** House of Troy, houseoftroy.com
**Shutters:** reclaimed pine
**Sofa:** by Florence Knoll, knoll.com
**Leather Armchair:** Crate & Barrel, crateandbarrel.com

**Bar Cabinet:** Crate & Barrel, crateandbarrel.com
**Virso Table:** Nienkämper, nienkamper.com
**Bronze Figurative Sculpture (beside fireplace):** by Randy Jewart, austingreenart.org

## The Chinese-Red Retreat
### Ruthie Sommers + Luke McDonough—Pages 105–07
**Ceiling Paint:** Fine Paints of Europe "Rembrandt Yellow," finepaintsofeurope.com
**Carpet:** Melrose Carpet, melrosecarpet.com
**Window Treatments:** custom. Fabric by Christopher Farr Cloth, christopherfarrcloth.com
**Tufted Banquet:** custom
**Coffee Table:** found on Dixie Highway. Custom refinishing
**Floral Chair and Footstool:** antique
**Set of Green Velvet Chairs:** antique, jamesandjeffrey.com
**Set of Floral Chairs:** antique. Fabric by Claremont Furnishing Fabrics Company, claremontfurnishing.com
**Wall-Mounted Bookcase Lights:** Urban Archaeology, urbanarchaeology.com
**Tone-on-Tone Wall Fabric:** by Rogers and Goffigon, delanyandlong.com

## The Fairy-tale Living Room
### Michelle + Dave Kohanzo—Pages 108–09
**Tufted Leather Sofa:** 14th Street Vintage, etsy.com
**Rug:** Land of Nod, landofnod.com
**Red Wingback Chair:** Brimfield store, brimfieldus.com
**Gray Wingback Chair:** Etsy.com. Custom slipcover from Calico Corners, calicocorners.com
**Armchair:** Crate & Barrel, crateandbarrel.com. Swiss army blanket upholstery, vintage
**Coffee Table:** eBay.com. Map decoupage by homeowner
**Lucite Trunk:** Lovintagefinds, etsy.com
**Wallpaper:** Orla Kiely, orlakiely.com/usa
**Custom Lampshades:** Fondue, etsy.com
**Silver Lamps:** Restoration Hardware, restorationhardware.com
**Custom Roman Shades:** fabric from Spoonflower, spoonflower.com. Made by Windows by Melissa, etsy.com

## The Scandinavian Living Room
### Anne Ziegler + Scott Mason—Pages 110–13
**Glass-Top Side Table:** vintage, empiricstudio.com
**White Lounge Chair:** HD Buttercup, hdbuttercup.com
**Sofa:** Cisco Bothers, ciscobrothers.com
**Throw Pillows:** by Josef Frank, justscandinavian.com
**Coffee Table:** Dennis & Leen, dennisandleen.com
**Gold Milano Plate (on coffee table):** by En Soie, maxandmoritz-la.com

**Framed Vintage Botanical Print:** by Jung-Koch Quentell, johnderian.com
**Antique Industrial Side Table:** Penine Hart Antiques and Art, peninehart.com
**Curtains:** IKEA, ikea.com
**French Side Chairs and Woolies:** chairs are vintage. Woolies are IKEA, ikea.com
**Printed Armchair:** fabric by Josef Frank, justscandinavian.com
**White Pottery Collection:** Astier de Villatte, astierdevillatte.com
**Clear Console Table:** CB2, cb2.com

## The Hot & Cold Living Room
### Brenda + David Bergen—Pages 114–15
**Sofa:** Stitch, stitchchicago.com
**Chair and Ottoman:** Womb Chair by Eero Saarinen for Knoll, dwr.com
**Shaggy Rug:** Crate & Barrel, crateandbarrel.com
**Glass-Top Coffee Table:** Judith Racht Gallery, judithrachtgallery.wordpress.com
**Throw Pillows:** Room & Board, roomandboard.com
**Credenza:** West Elm, westelm.com
**Blue Print:** by David Burdeny, lumas.com
**Koi Print:** by Andrew Stewart
**Wall Sculpture:** Vitra Algue by Bouroullec, vitra.com
**White Wall Cabinets:** IKEA, ikea.com
**Fireplace Insert:** Amazon.com

## The '70s Living Room
### Laura Jay Freedman—Pages 116–17
**'70s Leather Armchairs:** by Gianfranco Frattin, 1stdibs.com
**Large Sheepskin Throws:** Costco, costco.com
**Coffee Table:** vintage from Pasadena Rose Bowl Flea Market, rgcshows.com
**Wall-Mounted Brass Light:** Galerie Half, galeriehalf.com
**Brutalist Table Lamp:** by Paul Evans
**Fluorescent "Lips" Light:** designed by homeowner
**'70s Burl Wood Credenza:** by Paul Evans
**Artwork (above credenza):** gift

## eating spaces

### The French Provençal Dining Room
### Deborah Nevins—Pages 120–23
**Dining Table:** designed by homeowner
**Dining Chairs:** antique German garden chairs from Montauk, NY
**Large Bookcase:** antique from Manhattan
**Industrial Lights (on bookcase):** found in Hudson, NY
**Artwork (on bookcase):** by Stephen Antonakos, stephenantonakos.com

### The Breakfast Nook
### Jessica + Scott Davis—Pages 124–25
**Wall Paint:** Sherwin-Williams "Dovetail," sherwin-williams.com
**Tripod Table:** West Elm, westelm.com
**Hamilton Bentwood Dining Chairs:** Home Decorators Collection, homedecorators.com

**Custom Bench Seat Cushion:** made from West Elm shower curtain fabric
**Throw Pillows:** Etsy.com
**Osgood Pendant Light:** Arteriors, arteriorshome.com
**Blinds:** Home Depot, homedepot.com

## The Glossy Cabin Dining Room
### Christopher Coleman + Angel Sanchez—Pages 126–27
**Dining Table:** made by homeowners
**Dining Chairs:** vintage; recovered in Holly Hunt fabric, hollyhunt.com
**Hammered Bronze Pendant Light:** one of a kind
**Console Table:** vintage from Neven & Neven, nevenmoderne.com

## The Farmhouse-in-a-Skyscraper Dining Room
### Moon Rhee + Heyja Do—Pages 128–29
**Vintage 150 Year-Old Table:** found in Texas
**Assorted Vintage Dining Chairs:** Dear: Rivington, dearrivington.com
**Vintage Pendant Light:** Dear: Rivington, dearrivington.com
**'40s Outdoor Theater Chairs:** Dear: Rivington, dearrivington.com

## The Roundabout Dining Room
### Laura Jay Freedman—Pages 130–31
**'30s Dining Table and Chairs:** by Karl Springer. Chairs from Pasadena Rose Bowl Flea Market, rgcshows.com. Table, gift
**Large Painting:** gift
**Vintage Light Fixture:** by Alvin Lustig, 1stdibs.com
**Gold Column Light:** vintage, 1stdibs.com

## The Dark Menagerie Dining Room
### Michele Varian + Brad Roberts—Pages 132–33
**Framed Gold Mirrors:** by Ria Charisse, michelevarian.com
**Wedding Portrait:** found in the apartment
**Wallpaper:** by Neisha Crosland, neishacrosland.com
**Vintage Dining Room Table:** antique, eBay.com
**Red Folding Chairs:** antique, frenchgeneral.com
**Throw Pillow:** by Michele Varian, michelevarian.com

## The Country Porch Dining Room
### Paige + Smoot Hull—Pages 134–35
**Dining Table:** made by homeowners. Tabletop, found. Antique table legs, roundtoptexasantiques.com
**Cage Pendant Light:** by John Petty Antiques, thevintageroundtop.com
**Vintage Wire Chairs:** updated with burlap seats, roundtoptexasantiques.com
**Bench:** custom by John Dahl, jdahlwoodworks.com
**White Dining Chairs:** vintage, roundtoptexasantiques.com

**The Fab Two-in-One Dining Room**
**Taylor Swaim—Pages 136–37**
**Chevron Rug:** Pottery Barn, potterybarn.com
**Industrial Coffee Table:** West Elm, westelm.com
**Velvet Sofa:** West Elm, westelm.com
**"London" and "New York" Throw Pillows:** Home Goods, homegoods.com
**Southwestern Tapestry Pillow:** Brooklyn Flea, brooklynflea.com
**Black Table Lamps:** Martha Stewart for Kmart, kmart.com
**Antler Chandelier:** antique from Indiana
**Curtains:** Target, target.com
**Dining Table and Matching Chairs:** antiques from Indiana
**Tufted Chairs:** Home Goods, homegoods.com
**Silver Votives:** West Elm, westelm.com
**Bar Table:** family heirloom. Annie Sloan paint, anniesloan.com
**White Bowl (with lemons on bar):** Home Goods, homegoods.com
**White Mason Jar (on bar):** Fishs Eddy, fishseddy.com
**Striped Straws (on bar):** Target, target.com

## kitchens

**Opener**
**Allison + Ryan Burke—Pages 138–39**
**Framed Artwork:** by Ryan Hennessee and OK Mountain Collective
**Bartable:** vintage
**Bar Stools:** vintage
**Floating Shelf (above stove):** vintage luggage rack from an old train, urbanremainschicago.com
**Retro Wall-Mounted Shelves:** vintage, urbanremainschicago.com
**Cabinet Paint:** Sherwin-Williams "Greenfield," sherwin-williams.com
**Countertops:** Caesarstone, caesarstoneus.com
**Dishes:** Heath Ceramics, heathceramics.com
**Rug:** Mad Mats, madmats.com

**The Retro Bright Kitchen**
**Judy Kameon + Erik Otsea—Pages 140–43**
**Rug:** Mosaik, e-mosaik.com
**Kitchen Table:** made by homeowners
**Kitchen Chairs:** vintage Danish dealer in Cathedral City, CA. Fabric from Diamond Foam & Fabric, diamondfoamandfabric.com
**Vintage Wedgewood Stove:** found on Craigslist and revamped by homeowners
**Cabinets:** teak veneer (cabinetry throughout the house). Built by homeowner
**Tile Backsplash:** Heath Ceramics, heathceramics.com
**Countertop:** Lagos Azul Limestone
**Capiz Pendant Lamp:** similar at Jonathan Adler, jonathanadler.com
**Ikat Bench:** Plain Air, plainair.com. Outdoor fabric by Perennials, perennialsfabrics.com
**Black Ceramic Vessel (on kitchen cabinet):** by Erik Otsea

**The Beach Cottage Kitchen**
**Christiane Lemieux + Joshua Young—Pages 144–45**
**Floating Shelves:** custom
**Butcher Block Countertops:** IKEA, ikea.com
**Cabinetry:** IKEA, ikea.com
**Owl Cookie Jar:** Anthropologie, anthropologie.com
**Artwork:** by Deborah Kass

**The Never-at-Rest Kitchen**
**Lulu Powers + Stephen Danelian—Pages 146–47**
**Cabinet Paint:** Benjamin Moore "Lucerne," benjaminmoore.com
**Hardware:** bought in Nantucket, MA
**Palmeral Wallpaper (in sitting room):** Walnut Wallpaper, walnutwallpaper.com
**Green Armchairs:** Nantucket Looms, nantucketlooms.com
**Patterned Footstool:** footstool from Pom Pom at Home, pompomathome.com. Fabric by Michael Levine fabric, lowpricefabric.com
**Pendant Light:** Urban Outfitters, uo.com
**Floor Lamps:** Ralph Lauren, ralphlauren.com

**The Neapolitan Kitchen**
**Michelle + Dave Kohanzo—Pages 150–51**
**Wall Paint:** Benjamin Moore "Milkyway," benjaminmoore.com
**Cabinet Paint:** Benjamin Moore "Sweet 16," benjaminmoore.com
**Hutch:** vintage
**Industrial Pendant Light:** Anthropologie, anthropologie.com
**Plaid Rug:** Land of Nod, landofnod.com
**Yellow Side Table:** vintage
**Gingham Window Treatments:** made by homeowner
**Retro Dishes:** Etsy.com

**The Western Soda-Fountain Kitchen**
**Susan + Kevin Lennon—Pages 152–53**
**Stools:** from a diner in Kansas
**Holophane Lights:** vintage
**Countertop:** poured concrete
**Cabinet Hardware:** Restoration Hardware, restorationhardware.com

**The Collector's Bazaar Kitchen**
**Michele Varian + Brad Roberts—Pages 154–57**
**Wall Paint:** Benjamin Moore "782 Blue Belle" in gloss, benjaminmoore.com
**Thornbird Wallpaper (by fireplace):** by Michele Varian, michelevarian.com
**Hanging Glassware:** antique European flycatchers
**Assorted Dishes:** Pearl River, pearlriver.com
**Metal "Pantry" Locker:** flea market in NYC
**Colorful Chopsticks:** Pearl River, pearlriver.com
**Cutting Boards:** assorted designers, michelevarian.com

**Antique Slipper Chairs:** inherited from neighbor
**Wooden Radio:** Areaware, michelevarian.com

**The Smart-Storage Kitchen**
**Lisa + Joel Santos—Pages 158–61**
**Marquee "S" Light:** Hearts Desire in La Grange, IL
**Metal Hanging Utensil Rail:** Rosle, surlatable.com
**Task Light:** Prouvé Potence Lamp, dwr.com
**Stainless Steel Cabinetry:** IKEA, ikea.com
**Wall Cabinetry:** IKEA, ikea.com
**Dining Table:** Ravenswood Antique Mart, ravenswoodantiquemart.com
**Dining Chairs:** Eames Molded Plywood Dining Chairs, dwr.com

**The Little Kitchen That Could**
**Tim Cuppett + Marco Rini—Pages 162–65**
**Wall Paint Color:** Benjamin Moore "Gettysburg Gray," benjaminmoore.com
**Built-In Shelf Paint Color:** Benjamin Moore "Land of Liberty," benjaminmoore.com
**Wood Media Cabinet:** Crate & Barrel, crateandbarrel.com. Topped with Carrera marble
**Stainless Steel Counters:** local kitchen equipment company
**Striped Rug:** JM Drygoods, jmdrygoods.com
**Rolling Library Ladder:** Putnam Rolling Ladder, putnamrollingladder.com
**Tolomeo Sconces (mounted upside down):** Artemide, artemide.us
**Suspended Plate Rack:** designed by homeowner

**The Carefully Curated Kitchen**
**Emily Johnston—Pages 166–69**
**Wall Paint:** Benjamin Moore "Ice Storm," benjaminmoore.com
**Clear Storage Jars:** IKEA, ikea.com
**Industrial Pendant Light (over table):** West Elm, westelm.com
**Lantern Pendant Light (in center of room):** IKEA, ikea.com
**Screw-Top Dining Table:** Tom Dixon, tomdixon.net
**Dining Chairs:** Room & Board, roomandboard.com
**Framed Photograph:** by Emily Johnston
**Runner:** Heirloom Rug, heirloomrug.com
**Curved Porcelain Plates:** by Virginia Sin, virginiasin.com
**Hanging Utensil Storage:** IKEA, ikea.com

**The DIY Kitchen**
**Taylor Swaim—Pages 170–71**
**Kitchen Cabinet Makeover:** Rust-Oleum Cabinet Transformations Kit, rustoleumtransformations.com
**Faux Tin Backsplash Panels:** Home Depot, homedepot.com
**Kitchen Light:** Home Depot, homedepot.com

## work spaces

**The Closet-Office**
**Emily Johnston—Pages 174–77**
**Wall Paint:** Benjamin Moore "Storm Cloud Gray," benjaminmoore.com
**Hide Rug:** IKEA, ikea.com
**Silver Metal File Cabinet:** Bisley, bisleyusa.com
**Gray Metal File Cabinet:** CB2, cb2.com
**Industrial Green Desk Lamp:** vintage
**White Table Lamp:** CB2, cb2.com
**Desk Chair:** Room & Board, roomandboard.com
**Storage Boxes (in closet):** MUJI, muji.us

**A Color-Coded Office**
**Brenda + David Bergen—Pages 178–79**
**Green and White Storage Boxes:** The Container Store, containerstore.com
**Wooden Storage Boxes:** IKEA, ikea.com
**Desk:** made by homeowner

**The Den of Creativity**
**Moon Rhee + Heyja Do—Pages 180–81**
**Wooden Table:** vintage
**Fabric-Top Folding Computer Table:** vintage from Dear: Rivington, dearrivington.com
**Decorative Storage Buckets:** vintage, collected in Paris and Berlin
**Iron Collection:** vintage
**Metal Storage Baskets and Bookcase:** vintage, found at a school in New Orleans
**Plastic Egg Chair:** by Arne Jacobsen
**Rug:** vintage from the '70s

**The Sun Porch–Turned-Office**
**Anne Ziegler + Scott Mason—Pages 182–83**
**Work Tables:** IKEA, ikea.com
**Plastic Egg Chair:** by Arne Jacobsen, DWR.com
**Jieldé Desk Lamp:** Empiric, empiricstudio.com
**Printed Armchair:** fabric by Josef Frank, justscandinavian.com
**Stackable Powder-Coated Steel Trays:** Kaleido Trays, aplusrstore.com

**An Office with a View**
**Christopher Coleman + Angel Sanchez—Pages 184–85**
**Blonde Wood Desk:** vintage from Neven & Neven, nevenmoderne.com
**Rattan Chair:** Bielecky Brothers, bieleckybrothers.com
**'50s French Wall-Mounted Light Fixture:** vintage
**Framed Print:** silkscreen fabric sample
**Painted Canvas:** bought in Marfa, TX

**The Artist's Worktable**
**Michele Varian + Brad Roberts—Pages 186–87**
**Table:** vintage
**Throw Pillows:** by Michele Varian, michelevarian.com
**Curtains:** made by homeowner

## bedrooms

**Opener**
**Deborah Nevins—Pages 188–89**
**Twin Bed Frames:** antique folding French campaign beds
**French Bedding:** antique from London
**Side Tables:** custom
**Striped Rug:** Bloom in Sag Harbor, NY
**Wall Sconces:** designed by homeowner. Fabricated by Grand Brass, grandbrass.com
**Window Hardware:** Crown City, restoration.com

**A Novel Bedroom**
**Taylor Swaim—Pages 190–93**
**Raw Wood Frames:** Target, target.com
**Polka Dot Sheets:** Ralph Lauren, tjmaxx.com
**White Knotted Duvet:** DKNY, dkny.com
**Plaid Wool Throw Blanket:** Ralph Lauren, tjmaxx.com
**Mirrored Lamps:** Martha Stewart for Kmart, kmart.com
**Side Table:** antique from Indiana
**Rug:** TJ Maxx, tjmaxx.com
**Antique Typewriter (on desk):** family heirloom
**Papier-Mâché Deer Head:** West Elm, westelm.com
**Tufted Desk Chair:** Home Goods, homegoods.com

**The Surf Shack Bedroom**
**Susan + Kevin Lennon—Pages 194–95**
**Duvet and Shams:** IKEA, ikea.com
**Stitched Pillows:** Pottery Barn, potterybarn.com
**Quilt:** vintage African sari
**Lamp:** estate sale, revamped by homeowner
**Iron Bedframe:** vintage from Texas
**Floors:** painted plywood

**The Dark & Cozy Hideout**
**Emily Johnston—Pages 196–97**
**Hammock:** bought in France
**Light Fixture:** eBay.com
**Curtains:** West Elm, westelm.com
**Blanket:** Poglia & Co., poglia.co
**Splattered Pillowcases:** by Rebecca Atwood, rebeccaatwood.com

**The Garden View Bedroom**
**Deborah Nevins—Pages 198–99**
**Bedframe:** antique store in Rhinebeck, NY
**French Bedding:** antique from London
**Folding Table/Desk:** antique store in New Haven, NY
**Tolomeo Desk Light:** DWR, dwr.com
**Rug:** vintage Native American
**Framed Painting (homeowner at 14 years-old):** by Nancy Ransom
**Bedside Table:** flea market in East Hampton, NY
**Wall Sconces:** designed by homeowner. Fabricated by Grand Brass, grandbrass.com
**Window Hardware:** Crown City, restoration.com

**The Old Hollywood Bedroom**
**Lulu Powers + Stephen Danelian—Pages 200–01**
**Wallpaper:** by Pierre Deux
**Rattan Luggage:** vintage
**Bedding:** Lands' End, landsend.com
**Throw Pillows (on bed):** Nantucket Monogram, nantucketmonogram.com

**The French Boudoir**
**Ruthie Sommers + Luke McDonough—Pages 202–03**
**Carpet:** Stark Carpet, melrosecarpet.com
**Hand-Painted 'Askew' Wallpaper:** De Gournay, degournay.com
**19th Century Iron Canopy Bed:** Restoration Hardware, restorationhardware.com
**Curtains:** custom by Claudia Design Unlimited. Fabric by The Silk Trading Co., silktrading.com
**Dresser:** Paul Marra, paulmarradesign.com
**Table Lamps and Shades:** Sotheby's auction, sothebys.com

**The Blissed-Out Master Suite**
**Eric Oliver + Thea Goodman—Pages 204–05**
**Lilac Rug:** Madeline Weinrib, madelineweinrib.com
**Velvet Tufted Woodhouse Headboard:** Jonathan Adler, jonathanadler.com
**Table Lamps:** White Attic in Andersonville, IL, whiteattic.com
**Roman Shades:** Smith + Noble, smithandnoble.com
**White Dressers:** Jonathan Adler, jonathanadler.com
**Abbott Armchair:** Room & Board, roomandboard.com
**Mirrored Side Table:** Horchow, horchow.com

**The World-of-Whimsy Bedroom**
**Michelle + Dave Kohanzo—Pages 206–07**
**Wall Paint:** Benjamin Moore "Morning Sky," benjaminmoore.com
**Italian Campaign Canopy Bed:** Anthropologie, anthropologie.com
**City Quilt (on bed):** Haptic Labs, hapticlab.com
**Furry Throw Pillows (on bed):** West Elm, westelm.com
**Knit Throw Pillows (on bed):** Ralph Lauren, ralphlauren.com
**Eden Table Lamps:** Land of Nod, landofnod.com
**Round Side Table:** vintage
**Pink Chair:** Salvation Army, salvationarmyusa.org. Upholstered with Cath Kidston fabric, cathkidston.com
**Wall Mirror:** vintage
**Velvet Settee:** vintage
**Rags to Riches Rug:** Land of Nod, landofnod.com
**Folding Chair (holding blankets):** vintage from Wrigley Field
**German Movie Poster:** vintage
**Herringbone Storage Basket:** Land of Nod, landofnod.com

**Footstool:** vintage. Upholstered with Cath Kidston fabric, cathkidston.com

### The Minimalist Master Suite
**Moon Rhee + Heyja Do—Pages 208–09**
**Side Table:** antique from Kenya
**Victorian Lace Throw:** antique from the early 1890s
**Pillows:** vintage
**Painting:** by Moon Rhee

### The Stargazer's Lounge
**Tim Cuppett + Marco Rini—Pages 210–11**
**Wall Paint Color:** Benjamin Moore "Gettysburg Gray," benjaminmoore.com
**Hanging Bell Jar Pendant Light:** designed by homeowner. Fabricated by Brady's Distinctive Lighting, bradysdistinctivelighting.com
**Black Walnut and Pecan Wood Night Stands:** design by homeowner. Fabricated by Ambrose Taylor, austinartisan.org
**Hickory Headboard:** vintage from an old summer camp in East Texas
**Bedding:** Pottery Barn, potterybarn.com
**Striped Throw:** JM Drygoods, jmdrygoods.com

## kids' spaces

### A Bedroom Built for Three
**Michelle + Dave Kohanzo—Pages 214–17**
**Twin Bedframe (in middle):** antique from Brimfield Store, brimfielduc.com
**Simple Bunk (separated into two twin beds):** Land of Nod, landofnod.com
**Bedding:** Land of Nod, landofnod.com
**Wallpapered Maps:** collection of *National Geographic* maps adhered with wallpaper paste
**Mounted Fish:** Etsy.com
**Clip Light (attached to bed):** Land of Nod, landofnod.com
**Checkered Curtains:** Land of Nod, landofnod.com

### The Pretty-in-Pink Bedroom
**Mary + Lou Castelli—Pages 218–19**
**Headboard:** custom
**Bedding:** IKEA, ikea.com
**Wallpaper:** Graham & Brown, grahambrown.com
**Roman Shades:** illustration by Saul Steinberg, fschumacher.com

### The Superhero Bedroom
**Eric Oliver + Thea Goodman—Page 220–21**
**Headboard:** Land of Nod, landofnod.com
**Rug:** family heirloom
**Faux Sheepskin Rug:** IKEA, ikea.com
**Bedding:** Land of Nod, landofnod.com
**Quilt (with planes):** vintage
**Craft Table and Chairs:** IKEA, ikea.com

### The Sophisticated Nursery
**Jessica + Scott Davis—Pages 222–23**
**Wall Paint:** Sherwin-Williams "Repose Gray," sherwin-williams.com
**Rug:** vintage, esalerugs.com
**Curtains:** made by homeowner. Fabric: Spoonflower, spoonflower.com
**Crib:** WalMart, walmart.com
**Bed Skirt:** Land of Nod, landofnod.com
**Sheets:** New Mom Designs, etsy.com
**Hanging "Mobil:"** by Janelle Gramling, janellegramling.com
**Fasciati Glass Lantern:** Shades of Light, shadesoflight.com
**Framed Bear Print:** by Leah Duncan, leahduncan.com
**Framed Bird Prints:** by Charley Harper
**Dip-Dyed Wicker Basket:** basket from Target, target.com. Hand-painted by homeowner

### The Busy-Princess Retreat
**Maxwell Ryan—Pages 224–25**
**Wall Paint:** Farrow and Ball "Calluna," farrow-ball.com
**Bed with Built-in Storage:** Urban Homecraft, urbanhomecraft.com
**Bedding:** Dwell Studio in Penant, dwellstudio.com
**Bedside Light:** IKEA, ikea.com
**Hanging Canopy:** 100% Cotton Canopy, nicamaka.com
**Shearling Rug:** ABC Carpet & Home, abchome.com

### Craft Nook
**Wall Paint:** Farrow and Ball "Lulworth Blue," farrow-ball.com
**Vintage Mirror:** Bobo Intriguing Objects, bobointriguingobjects.com
**Desk:** IKEA, ikea.com
**Metal Shelf:** Lambertson, lambertson.com
**Wall-Mounted Book Shelf:** Artek Wall Shelf, artek.fi
**Sewing Machine:** IKEA, ikea.com
**Striped Rug:** Surya, surya.com

### The Tree-House Bedroom
**Christiane Lemieux + Joshua Young—Pages 226–27**
**Bunk Beds:** custom
**Bedding:** Dwell Studio, dwellstudio.com
**Roman Shades:** Dwell Studio for The Shade Store, theshadestore.com
**Papier-Mâché Zebra Head:** Dwell Studio, dwellstudio.com
**Framed Prints:** Natural Curiosities, naturalcuriosities.com
**Toy Store:** storage by Oeuf, dwellstudio.com
**Garland Light:** by Tord Boontje, wayfair.com

### The LEGO Lair
**Brenda + David Bergen—Pages 228–29**
**Moda Loft Bed and Desk:** Room & Board, roomandboard.com
**Hanging Ship:** bought in Bali

**Bedding:** Restoration Hardware, restorationhardware.com
**Purple Felt Toy Bins:** Land of Nod, landofnod.com
**Desk Chair:** IKEA, ikea.com

### Her Highness's Alcove
**Ruthie Sommers + Luke McDonough—Pages 230–31**
**Dresser:** thrift store
**Table Lamp:** antique from Shi & Erhard in West Palm Beach, FL
**Sheets:** Schweitzer Linen, schweitzerlinen.com
**Window Valance (used as canopy):** Pindler & Pindler, pindler.com
**Curtain Fabric:** Pindler & Pindler, pindler.com

## bathrooms

### Opener
**Christiane Lemieux + Joshua Young—Pages 232–33**
**Wall Paint Color:** Benjamin Moore "Blue Aqua," benjaminmoore.com
**Soap Bowl:** Iittala Taika bowl, iittala.com
**Mercury Candle Votives:** Canvas Home, canvashomestore.com
**Sink:** IKEA, ikea.com

### The Indoor/Outdoor Bathroom
**Susan + Kevin Lennon—Pages 234–37**
**Outdoor Shower Walls:** reclaimed house siding and windows
**Sink:** estate sale in Petaluma, CA
**Toilet:** salvage yard in LA
**Mirror (next to toilet):** flea market in New York

### The Art Deco Bathroom
**Laura Jay Freedman—Pages 238–39**
**Art Deco Mirror (over toilet):** vintage from Pasadena Rose Bowl Flea Market, rgcshows.com
**Mirrored Trash Bin:** eBay.com
**Striped Robe:** Ace Hotel, shop.acehotel.com

### The Dark Spa Retreat
**Lulu Powers + Stephen Danelian—Pages 240–41**
**Wallpaper:** Walnut Wallpapers, walnutwallpaper.com
**Floor Tile:** Walker Zanger, walkerzanger.com
**Vanity:** antique shop in Memphis, TN
**Mirror (above vanity):** antique shop in Memphis, TN
**Cabinet:** vintage
**Bathroom Fixtures:** Lefroy Brooks, lefroybrooks.com

### The Breezy Beach House Bathroom
**Deborah Nevins—Pages 242–43**
**Floor Paint:** Pratt & Lambert Paints, prattandlambert.com
**Sink:** salvage from the Lexington Armory Show
**Towel Rack:** flea market
**Tri-Mirror:** flea market

Wall-Mounted Vanity Mirror: flea market
Shutters (as closet doors): flea market

### The *Old Man and the Sea* Bathroom
**Taylor Swaim—Pages 244–45**
**Wall Paint:** Behr "Intellectual," behr.com
**Anchor Towel Rack:** West Elm, westelm.com
**White Frames:** IKEA, ikea.com
**Hand Towels:** West Elm, westelm.com
**Silver Tray (on toilet):** antique
**Hand Soaps:** West Elm, westelm.com

### The Modern '80s Bathroom
**Mary + Lou Castelli—Pages 246–47**

**Powder Room**
**Yellow Tile:** Trend, annsacks.com
**Sink:** Lacava, lacava.com
**Knobble Mirror:** Y Living, yliving.com
**Towel Hook:** by Josh Owen, kontextur.com

**Kid's Washroom**
**Tile:** Nemo Tile, nemotile.com
**Pendant Lights:** Y Lighting, ylighting.com
**Roman Shade:** custom

### The Zen Garden Retreat
**Susan + Kevin Lennon—Pages 248–49**
**Bathtub:** Tea for Two by Kohler, us.kohler.com
**Shower Tiles:** Hokati Glass Tiles

## outdoor spaces

### The Plant Whisperer's Wonderland
**Judy Kameon + Erik Otsea—Pages 252–55**
**Table:** Plain Air, plainair.com
**Chairs:** Plain Air, plainair.com. Ikat Outdoor Fabric: by Perennials, perennialsfabrics.com
**Benches:** Plain Air, plainair.com. Striped Outdoor Fabric: by Perennials, perennialsfabrics.com
**Camping Plates:** Broadway Panhandler, broadwaypanhandler.com
**Cloth Napkins:** Les Toiles du Soleil, lestoilesdusoleilnyc.com
**Succulent Planter:** Bauer Pottery, bauerpottery.com
**Chandeliers (in tree):** vintage

### The Family Deck
**Susan + Kevin Lennon—Pages 256–59**
**Table:** made by homeowner
**Bench:** made from vintage scaffold board
**Outdoor Cushions and Pillows:** made by homeowner from vintage mailbags, military bags, and ticking fabric
**Planters:** vintage lamp posts cut to create planters
**Couch:** made by homeowner from vintage metal skids

### The Nature Observatory
**Christopher Coleman + Angel Sanchez—Pages 260–61**
**Exterior House Paint:** Benjamin Moore "Black Forest Green," benjaminmoore.com
**Crow Collection:** collected while traveling
**Hide Rug:** street vendor in LA
**Armchair:** from Doyle New York, doylenewyork.com. Recovered in custom fabric
**Sofa:** B&B Italia Sleep Sofa, bebitalia.com
**Throw Pillows:** Home Nature, homenature.com
**Wall-Mounted Lights:** Artemide, artemide.us

### The Chauffeur's Garden Estate
**Ruthie Sommers + Luke McDonough—Pages 262–65**
**Marble Dining Table:** Rubbish Interiors, rubbishinteriors.com
**Dining Chairs:** vintage, casavictoriala.com
**Hammock:** Pawleys Island Hammock Shop, pawleysislandhammocks.com
**Pink Plates with Gold Trim:** Anna Weatherley, scullyandscully.com
**Scrolling Iron Settee (by pool):** antique, pasadenaantiquecenter.com

### A Sunny Scrap of Patio
**Laura Jay Freedman—Pages 266–67**
**Table:** Pasadena Rose Bowl Flea Market, rgcshows.com

### The Texas-Style Front Porch
**Paige + Smoot Hull—Pages 268–69**
**Picnic Table and Bench:** garage sale
**Red Folding Chairs:** vintage from Round Top Antiques Fair, roundtoptexasantiques.com
**Throw Pillows:** Kuhl-Linscomb, kuhllinscomb.com
**Rocking Chair:** garage sale

**Carrom Gameboard:** vintage, vintageroundtop.com
**Globe Light Strings:** Target, target.com
**Porch Swing (on tree):** came with house

### An Alfresco Dining Spot in the Hills
**Anne Ziegler + Scott Mason—Pages 270–71**
**Table and Chairs:** came with the house
**Cashmere Throw Blankets:** West Elm, westelm.com
**White Plates:** CB2, cb2.com
**Gray Plates:** Mud Australia, mudaustralia.com
**Striped Cloth Napkins:** John Robshaw, johnrobshaw.com
**Water Pitcher:** Jenni Kayne Home, jennikayne.com
**Military Cot:** vintage
**Throwbed Cushion (on cot):** Hedgehouse, hedgehouseusa.com
**Pillow (on cot):** bought in Mexico

### The Easy English Garden
**Tim Cuppett + Marco Rini—Pages 272–73**
**Water Silo (in the backyard):** Timber Tanks, timbertanks.com

### The Urban Jungle
**Lulu Powers + Stephen Danelian—Pages 274–75**
**Striped Gazebo:** custom
**Sofa and Chairs:** Oasis, oasisimports.com
**Orange and White Throw Pillows:** custom
**Coffee Table:** vintage
**Orange Side Tables:** Oasis, oasisimports.com
**Table Lamp:** gift

## PART THREE
## maintaining your home
**Lisa + Joel Santos—Pages 276–77**
**Wardrobe Closets:** IKEA, ikea.com

## repairs

**Judy Kameon + Erik Otsea—Page 288**
**Vintage O'Keefe & Merritt Stove:** Antique Stove Heaven, antiquestoveheaven.com

# acknowledgments . . .

**Our thanks & gratitude to:**

All of the folks who opened their doors to us, allowing us to spend long days capturing the beauty of their homes, and for believing in our mission—that this sharing of ideas would help others.

Our editorial team—Adrienne, Carrie, Dabney, Jennifer, and Nancy—for brainstorming the original idea, knowing what was important to communicate, and contributing their personal experience and compelling voices to the first and last sections.

Melanie Acevedo, for the artistry of her camera and for putting up with us as we took thousands of photographs in search of the perfect ones. All of the stylists who helped to make each and every photo beautiful: Olga Naiman (NYC), Kevin Hertzog (NYC), Kate Jordan (NYC), Beckel Cook (LA), Alicia Blais (Chicago), and Crisman Liverman (Austin). And the photo assistants who went above and beyond the call of duty: Paul Fittipaldi (NYC), Chris Davis (NYC), Brian Pietrini (Chicago), and Matthew Johnson (Austin).

Meghann Stephenson, for bringing a bright, cheerful playfulness to our pages with her beautiful watercolor illustrations.

Aliza Fogelson, for standing behind us at Potter Style and painstakingly editing all of our words, arranging them into a better and more compelling order. Ashley Tucker and Marysarah Quinn's collective efforts in dreaming up a design that jumps off the page. Doris Cooper for her support and guidance.

Kari Stuart and Andrea Barzvi at ICM, for helping us to launch this project, and Ashley Anderson, for helping to keep it on track before . . .

. . . Heather Summerville arrived to lead the project, adding sophistication, patience, judgment, and an overall commitment to excellence that formed our great idea into the biggest and best book we've ever accomplished.

# index

Page references in *italics* refer to illustrations.